Beyond Borders

Viewpoints/Puntos de Vista
Themes and Interpretations in Latin American History

Series editor: Jürgen Buchenau

The books in this series will introduce students to the most significant themes and topics in Latin American history. They represent a novel approach to designing supplementary texts for this growing market. Intended as supplementary textbooks, the books will also discuss the ways in which historians have interpreted these themes and topics, thus demonstrating to students that our understanding of our past is constantly changing, through the emergence of new sources, methodologies, and historical theories. Unlike monographs, the books in this series will be broad in scope and written in a style accessible to undergraduates.

Published

In preparation

Beyond Borders

A History of Mexican Migration to the United States

Timothy J. Henderson

A John Wiley & Sons, Ltd., Publication

This edition first published 2011
© Timothy J. Henderson

Blackwell Publishing was acquired by John Wiley & Sons in February 2007. Blackwell's publishing program has been merged with Wiley's global Scientific, Technical, and Medical business to form Wiley-Blackwell.

Registered Office
John Wiley & Sons Ltd, The Atrium, Southern Gate, Chichester, West Sussex, PO19 8SQ, United Kingdom

Editorial Offices
350 Main Street, Malden, MA 02148-5020, USA
9600 Garsington Road, Oxford, OX4 2DQ, UK
The Atrium, Southern Gate, Chichester, West Sussex, PO19 8SQ, UK

For details of our global editorial offices, for customer services, and for information about how to apply for permission to reuse the copyright material in this book please see our website at www.wiley.com/wiley-blackwell.

The right of Timothy J. Henderson to be identified as the author of this work has been asserted in accordance with the UK Copyright, Designs and Patents Act 1988.

Wiley also publishes its books in a variety of electronic formats. Some content that appears in print may not be available in electronic books.

Designations used by companies to distinguish their products are often claimed as trademarks. All brand names and product names used in this book are trade names, service marks, trademarks or registered trademarks of their respective owners. The publisher is not associated with any product or vendor mentioned in this book. This publication is designed to provide accurate and authoritative information in regard to the subject matter covered. It is sold on the understanding that the publisher is not engaged in rendering professional services. If professional advice or other expert assistance is required, the services of a competent professional should be sought.

Library of Congress Cataloging-in-Publication Data
Henderson, Timothy J.
  Beyond borders : a history of Mexican migration to the United States / Timothy J. Henderson.
    p. cm.
  Includes bibliographical references and index.
  ISBN 978-1-4051-9429-7 (hardcover : alk. paper) -- ISBN 978-1-4051-9430-3 (pbk. : alk. paper) 1. United States--Emigration and immigration--History. 2. Mexico--Emigration and immigration--History. 3. Mexicans--United States--History. 4. United States--Relations--Mexico. 5. Mexico--Relations--United States. I. Title.
  JV6895.M48H46 2010
  304.8'73072--dc22
                                                                                    2010038164

A catalogue record for this book is available from the British Library.

Set in 10 on 12.5 pt Minion by Toppan Best-set Premedia Limited
Printed in Malaysia by Ho Printing (M) Sdn Bhd

01   2011

Contents

List of Figures

Series Editor's Preface

Each book in the "Viewpoints/Puntos de Vista" series introduces students to a significant theme or topic in Latin American history. In an age in which student and faculty interest in the developing world increasingly challenges the old focus on the history of Europe and North America, Latin American history has assumed an increasingly prominent position in undergraduate curricula.

Some of these books discuss the ways in which historians have interpreted these themes and topics, thus demonstrating that our understanding of our past is constantly changing, through the emergence of new sources, methodologies, and historical theories. Others offer an introduction to a particular theme by means of a case study or biography in a manner easily understood by the contemporary, non-specialist reader. Yet others give an overview of a major theme that might serve as the foundation of an upper-level course.

What is common to all of these books is their goal of historical synthesis by drawing on the insights of generations of scholarship on the most enduring and fascinating issues in Latin American history, and through the use of primary sources as appropriate. Each book is written by a specialist in Latin American history who is concerned with undergraduate teaching, yet who has also made his or her mark as a first-rate scholar.

The books in this series can be used in a variety of ways, recognizing the differences in teaching conditions at small liberal arts colleges, large public universities, and research-oriented institutions with doctoral programs. Faculty have particular needs depending on whether they teach large lectures with discussion sections, small lecture or discussion-oriented classes, or large lectures with no discussion sections, and whether they teach on a semester or trimester system. The format adopted for this series fits all of these different parameters.

In this third volume in the "Viewpoints/Puntos de Vista" series, Timothy Henderson analyzes the history of Mexican immigration into the United States from its origins to the present day. This pattern of immigration is unique in that the territory of the United States includes half of what was once Mexico. Hence, successive waves of immigrants built on a base of approximately 100,000 Mexicans included in the borders of the United States pursuant to the 1848 Treaty of Guadalupe Hidalgo. As a result, the US–Mexican border region has long enjoyed a bicultural flavor, and Mexican influences in the US Southwest have always been strong.

Henderson's book looks at the factors on both sides of the border that have transplanted millions of Mexicans across that border and into a nation that now boasts a population of Mexican immigrants and US citizens of Mexican descent that is approaching 25 million. Almost 7 million are undocumented immigrants, often described as "illegal aliens" in US media. These undocumented Mexicans – almost 60 percent of all undocumented immigrants in the United States – are at the center of a passionate and emotionally charged debate. Henderson's work gives the reader a profound historical sense of how the Mexican population in the United States has evolved over time, and how this population has helped define the United States, Mexico, and the relationship between these two neighboring nations.

Jurgen Buchenau
University of North Carolina, Charlotte

Acknowledgments

This book does not claim to contribute original research. It owes a tremendous debt to the historians and journalists who have done exhaustive research over the years and published their findings. The ones I have relied on most are listed under "Further Reading." My profound thanks to all those authors, and I trust it is understood that any errors of fact or interpretation are my own.

Thanks to the inter-library loan folks at Auburn University Montgomery, and to my colleagues in the History Department. I am, as always, grateful to my wife, Karren Pell, for proofreading and offering advice on the manuscript, vastly improving the book in the process. Thanks also to two anonymous readers for Wiley-Blackwell, who read the manuscript with great care and contributed many valuable suggestions. My thanks also to Peter Coveney at Wiley-Blackwell, to editorial assistant Galen Smith, and to series editor (and friend of long standing) Jurgen Buchenau.

Migration is a failure of roots. Displaced men are ecological victims. Between them and the sustaining earth a wedge has been driven. Eviction by droughts or dispossession by landlords, the impoverishment of the soil or conquest by arms – nature and man, separately or together, lay down the choice: move or die. Those who are able to break away do so, leaving a hostile world behind to face an uncertain one ahead.

Ernesto Galarza, Merchants of Labor

To be hungry is human. To have papers or not to have papers is inhuman. It is against nature's laws. That's the point. There is a good reason for being the way he is. The state cannot make use of human beings. It would cease to exist. Human beings only make trouble. Men cut out of cardboard do not make trouble. Yesser. Excuse me, I mean: yes, sir.

B. Traven, The Death Ship

Introduction

A mong the hundreds of thousands of people who cross surrep-
titiously into the United States each year, Mexicans enjoy the
distinction of being the only ones whose nationality is mentioned by
name in official documents. All the rest, no matter where in the world
they hail from, are lumped into the unglamorous category of "Other
Than Mexicans," or "OTMs" in Border Patrol parlance.

The reason is obvious: Mexicans make up about 93 percent of those
surreptitious border crossers. Anyone picking up this book is surely well
aware that migration from Mexico is, and has long been, a "hot button
issue." Immigration in general has always been irresistible to demagogues, for it involves, or is perceived to involve, vital matters such as
race and ethnicity, nationality, national security, language, culture, economics, health, law, and community. Those whose personal or political
interests are served by igniting fear and hatred have always found immigrants to be convenient targets. Anti-immigrant activists condemn
immigrants as strangers among us, inscrutable "others" invading our
safe, comfortable, homogeneous spaces, burdening budgets, spreading
crime and disease, refusing to learn "our language" or to practice "our
ways."

Mexicans are merely the latest immigrants to receive such treatment,
but they are by no means alone. In a letter dated 1753, no less a

Beyond Borders: A History of Mexican Migration to the United States
By Timothy J. Henderson
© 2011 Timothy J. Henderson

figure than Benjamin Franklin vented against German immigrants to Pennsylvania, calling them "ignorant," "stupid," "swarthy," and a threat to American culture and freedom. Similar scorn has, throughout American history, been heaped upon the Irish, Italians, Spaniards, Jews, Catholics, Slavs, Asians, Africans, Muslims – that is, virtually every group of people that has alighted on these shores in numbers large enough to get themselves noticed. American history is punctuated with "nativist" movements, that is, movements that seek to privilege the interests of the native born over those of immigrants. A great irony of American life is that each generation of nativists are themselves likely the descendants of immigrants, who may have been reviled by unwelcoming citizens in an earlier day.

Immigrants from Mexico share many similarities with other immigrants. Mexicans migrate to the United States for roughly the same reasons as other immigrants: they might wish to join family members, have a lust for adventure, or need to escape something in their home country; but mostly they need jobs, which are scarce back home. Also, even though critics are fond of accusing Mexicans of refusing to assimilate to American culture, this same accusation has been made about every immigrant group at some point in history (one of Ben Franklin's chief complaints about the Germans, for instance, was that they refused to learn English). Studies have shown repeatedly that, all things being equal, Mexicans fully integrate into American society within two or three generations, which is identical to the integration rate for other immigrant groups.

But, in fact, all things are not equal. Immigration from Mexico differs from other immigration in several crucial ways. For one thing, a large portion of the United States once belonged to Mexico, and that portion was taken from Mexico in a war that even a patriot like Ulysses S. Grant described as "one of the most unjust ever waged by a stronger against a weaker nation."[1] At the end of that war, there were as many as 100,000 Mexicans living in the US Southwest, and this at a time when the overall population of that region was sparse. Mexican culture, as well as vigorous cross-border ties, has remained very much alive there. Although Mexican Americans were frequently victims of discrimination and violence, they have nevertheless been a part of American culture for more than a century and a half. The primordial relationship that Mexicans enjoy with the Southwest has allowed nationalistic Mexicans and Mexican Americans to claim that region as a sort of ancestral homeland, thus incurring the wrath of nativists. Parts of the Chicano movement of the 1960s and 1970s, for example, took to referring to the southwestern United States as "Aztlán," after the mythical homeland of the Aztecs. Some more radical elements postulated remaking the region into a new Mexican homeland, giving rise to persistent nativist charges that a conspiracy is afoot to "reconquer" that territory. Recently, nativist rage was provoked when a popular *norteño* band, Los Tigres del Norte, scored a hit with a song that briefly rehearsed the history of the US–Mexican War and concluded with the lyrics, "If you count the centuries, although it pains our neighbors, we are more American than all of the gringos." And in 2008 the Absolut vodka company was obliged to apologize for wounding American sensibilities with its ad depicting Mexico with its pre-1848 borders.

Mexican immigration is larger and more sustained than other immigrations. Although European immigration in the late nineteenth and early twentieth centuries was proportionately larger, substantial immigration from Mexico has gone on for about a century, and since the 1940s it has roughly doubled in every decade. Mexicans in the United States have congregated in such numbers that they have little incentive to assimilate to American culture. They can speak, eat, worship, and be entertained in the United States as if they were in Mexico. The Mexican economy in the United States is roughly the same size as the economy of Mexico.

But perhaps the most important difference between migration from Mexico and migration from other parts of the world is that so much of Mexican immigration has been categorized as "illegal." The taint of illegality has tended to keep a large portion of the Mexican population of the United States in the shadows, and it has slowed the integration of Mexicans to US culture. A conundrum has thus arisen, wherein American society criticizes Mexicans for failing to assimilate while simultaneously making it extraordinarily difficult for them to assimilate.

Nativist groups often portray Mexican immigrants as swarthy, impoverished hordes determined to partake of American prosperity, and they warn that tolerating such encroachments will lead ultimately to the impoverishment of the entire nation. This perspective ignores the considerable body of research – perhaps not definitive, but persuasive – making the case that Mexican workers have contributed far more to the American economy than they have taken away. It also ignores the topic of this book, namely, the *history* of Mexican immigration to the United States.

Illegal – and much legal – immigration from Mexico is a creature of American capitalism. Mexicans first began trekking northward because growers and other employers in the southwestern United States wanted easy and reliable access to cheap, expendable labor, and they were willing to do whatever it might take to hold on to a workforce that was both ample and poorly paid. In creating and maintaining that workforce, employers have frequently broken the law, or used their influence to have the law written to suit their needs and interests. In the early twentieth century, for example, when the migratory trend was still in its infancy, employers used Mexican labor contractors to lure Mexicans northward with offers of work, even though contract labor arrangements of this sort were illegal. During the 1940s, when the United States and Mexico had in place a program to bring Mexican guest workers into the United States to fill temporary agricultural jobs, many employers violated the law by employing both legal and illegal Mexican labor. Sometimes they even encouraged their legal workers to go back to Mexico and return to the United States illegally. They did this because the guest worker program guaranteed minimum wages and protections to *braceros* (as those guest workers were called). Illegal immigrants, by contrast, had no rights and no recourse. They could be underpaid or – in the case of some bottom-feeding employers – not paid at all. Many employers were quite frank in expressing their strong preference for illegal workers. Even when the US Congress passed a law in the 1950s declaring it a crime to "transport or harbor" an illegal immigrant, powerful interests saw to it that *employing* an illegal immigrant remained perfectly legal. And even today, when employing undocumented workers is technically illegal, employers run little risk.

Politicians have done their bit to maintain illegal flows. In the mid-1960s, Congress rewrote American immigration law. Prior to that rewriting, the nations of the world were assigned immigration quotas based on the racist assumptions of men who had reformed the immigration laws back in 1924. The 1965 law, in the name of fairness, assigned equal quotas to all of the nations of the earth, not taking into account the obvious fact that demand for visas was bound to be higher in some countries than in others. Suggestions that some exception should be made for "contiguous countries" – i.e., Canada and Mexico – were ignored. Moreover, preference was given for family reunification and for certain job skills that were deemed useful to the US economy. Later reforms only compounded these problems, meaning that for most ordinary Mexicans nowadays it is virtually impossible to migrate legally to the United States. And yet the lack of jobs in Mexico and the availability of jobs in the United States have made immigration practically inevitable and most likely unstoppable. Certainly, walls and fences – the latest craze – have proved ineffective and counterproductive.

According to the most commonly cited estimate, today there are roughly 12 million undocumented immigrants living in the United States, and about 60 percent of them are Mexicans. Attitudes toward these immigrants are varied. At one extreme are the seething xenophobes who would like to rid the country of foreigners once and for all. At another pole are those who insist that illegal immigration from Mexico is not really a problem, or that the problem is greatly exaggerated. After all, this argument runs, Mexicans only take jobs that Americans will not do; they help the economy by keeping down prices of food, restaurants, and hotels; the low wages they are paid help to keep some businesses in the United States that would otherwise relocate overseas; and most of them pay taxes and contribute to social security, while collecting few public services.

Although many who argue along these latter lines are well meaning, downplaying the evils of illegal immigration is unhelpful. Although there is ample and compelling evidence that undocumented immigrants are far less of a burden on American society than is often claimed – that is, that they do not compete for jobs, drive down wages, and use social services to such a great extent – that misses the point.[2] Surely society will always require low-paid work in many sectors of the economy, but there is no requirement that that work always be done by ethnic minorities. Maintaining such a large proportion of the Mexican population of the United States in an "illegal" status has a number of pernicious effects. It tends to reinforce the link between immigration and crime in the minds of many Americans, and hence places all Mexicans, whether in the country legally or illegally, at a disadvantage. It also impedes many Mexicans from following the course taken by earlier generations of immigrants, that is, settling down and working their way up in society. For the largest part of the history of Mexican immigration to the United States, migration was circular: Mexicans assumed that their sojourn in the United States would be temporary, so there was little incentive to put down roots. That has changed drastically since the immigration reform of 1986 and the tremendous buildup of border enforcement in the 1990s and early 2000s, which have persuaded more Mexicans to remain in the United States for the long haul, even if illegally. But the taint of illegality means that many Mexican immigrants are permanently stuck at the entry level, unable to work their way up through the proverbial ranks, afraid to join unions that might help to better their lot, unable to get health insurance or other social benefits, and with little incentive or opportunity to get an education – in general, unable to become fully integrated into American society on a basis of equality.[3] Maintaining a large, ethnically distinct population to do society's menial labor is hardly a sign of social health. And critics of illegal immigration have a good point when they note that, in a society that prides itself on its basis in the rule of law, tolerating widespread violation of the law by both immigrants and their employers is problematic.

Without a doubt, the strangest and most troubling feature of debates on Mexican immigration is the tendency to ignore Mexico, or to take Mexico into account only to lambaste it as a source of contagion. The overwhelming majority of books on Mexican immigration treat the issue as if it were an exclusively American problem – a problem that can eventually be solved if only we hit upon the right formula of tweaks and fixes. Cooperative solutions are seldom contemplated, though, to be sure, Mexico has not always proved an enthusiastic collaborator. Mexican leaders have traditionally viewed migration with great ambivalence. On the one hand, the money that emigrants send home has long been vital to Mexico's economy, and migration benefits Mexico in the sense that it is able to export a large part of its unemployment problem – about 10 percent of all Mexicans currently reside in the United States – and thus mitigate social unrest. On the other hand, Mexico's dependence on emigration to the United States has been deeply humiliating, a constant and poignant reminder of the nation's failure to realize the promises of its epic revolution of the early twentieth century. The "safety valve" effect of emigration has also probably been a factor enabling Mexican leaders to put off making reforms that are desperately needed. In the end, neither the United States nor Mexico really benefits from the prevailing situation.

It is often said that immigration involves both push and pull factors, and although that formulation has come in for some provocative criticism of late,[4] it nevertheless probably corresponds to the perception of most immigrants: they see themselves pushed by joblessness, violence, and poverty in their homeland, and pulled by the promise of relatively high-paying jobs on the other side of the border. To treat the matter as an exclusively American phenomenon – something that has wrongfully been inflicted upon the American people by a malignant and incomprehensible world beyond its borders – is to overlook the most important part of the equation. Trying to understand Mexican immigration without understanding something about Mexico is rather like trying to predict the weather with nothing but a weathervane, a thermometer, and a rain gauge. The only hope of resolving the problem is through real binational cooperation.

This book looks at Mexican migration from both sides of the border and over the course of the phenomenon's entire history. It seeks to explain the developments in the Mexican economy and society that have driven Mexicans to pull up stakes, most of them reluctantly, to undertake the hazardous journey north; and the ever-changing reception they have been accorded upon arrival on the other side of the border.

1

Beginnings

1848–1920

Mexicans began migrating to the United States in significant numbers in the early twentieth century, a time when both Mexico and the American Southwest were undergoing dramatic transformations. Although the character of Mexican migration to the United States has changed profoundly over the course of a century, the forces that drew Mexicans northward have remained essentially the same: Mexicans were enticed by American employers who offered them work for better wages than they could earn in Mexico; and they were propelled to leave by violence, poverty, and lack of opportunity in their homeland.

By the end of the second decade of the twentieth century, several enduring patterns had been established. American employers actively recruited Mexican workers when they were needed, but took no responsibility for them when the need decreased. Mexicans, who migrated from the neighboring country and could relatively easily be sent home, were an employer's dream: Mexicans were cheap and expendable, and, so long as labor unions or the US government did not interfere, they had little recourse to defend their rights and improve their lot. When the US economy slowed and jobs became scarce, Mexicans made handy scapegoats. The pattern of migration that developed was circular: Mexicans came and went, with relatively few choosing to settle permanently in the United States and assimilate to American culture.

Beyond Borders: A History of Mexican Migration to the United States
By Timothy J. Henderson
© 2011 Timothy J. Henderson

American capital, lured to Mexico by the enticements of cheap labor and raw materials, came to dominate the Mexican economy. That domination was an important factor retarding Mexico's economic development, for the chief lures attracting capital to Mexico have remained constant: cheap labor and resources. Mexico's leaders have added to the problem by making unwise choices with depressing regularity.

This chapter traces the beginnings of these enduring patterns.

How the Border Came to Be

In a sense, the first Mexicans to reside in the United States managed the remarkable feat of migrating without ever leaving home. Instead, the border of their country migrated to the south and west, landing them in a new and alien nation, one in which they quickly came to comprise a small and frequently persecuted minority. Their numbers are usually estimated between 80,000 and 100,000.

Understanding how and why that border readjustment came to pass requires at least a brief recounting of some deep history. From even before their respective foundings as colonies of European powers, Mexico and the United States developed very differently, and the differences tended overwhelmingly to favor the United States as the world entered into the "modern" era. Mexico – particularly its southern and central regions – was home to the populous and highly advanced indigenous civilizations of the Aztecs, Mayas, and a number of smaller groups. The Spaniards who arrived to conquer and colonize Mexico in 1519 found it neither possible nor desirable to eradicate or relocate such large numbers of Indians – although they did manage to kill off appalling numbers with a combination of over-exploitation and imported diseases – so they sought accommodations. Indians were cast in the role of peasants and workers, the lowest rung in what soon became a complex racial hierarchy. Indians were joined by Africans and persons of mixed race, known generically as "castes." By the time the Spanish colony came to an end in 1821, Mexico's population consisted of roughly 60 percent Indians, 22 percent castes, and 18 percent whites. Most Indians and castes were poor and illiterate; many could not speak or understand Spanish, which white elites insisted was the national tongue; and a long legacy of discrimination and exploitation, together with the practical impossibility of rising up the social ladder no matter how hard they worked, tended to give them a rather pessimistic worldview. White people, meanwhile, had a near monopoly on literacy, owned most of the wealth, and held virtually all of the political power. In short, Mexico's racial and class makeup was more complex than that of the United States, meaning ultimately that Mexico was forced to confront challenges that the United States was not obliged to face.

Race and class were not the only obstacles to Mexico's smooth entry into the modern world. A wealthy Catholic Church that wielded much political power and which had no intention of tolerating competing belief systems; a formidably rugged geography that made transportation and communication exceedingly difficult; a tendency for its people to fragment into isolated regional cultures; a long history of government by kings who claimed absolute power; and an economy that for three centuries had been a state monopoly that was obsessively focused on a single pursuit, the mining of silver: all of these factors combined to make Mexico's early years as a nation uncommonly difficult. Those years were characterized by extremes of penury and political turmoil, even while the United States grew in population and power, increasingly insisting that its "manifest destiny" was to control the North American continent in its entirety.

The United States, by contrast, was the spawn of Great Britain, the world's pioneer industrial nation. Great Britain was the world's greatest producing and trading nation in the late eighteenth century, and the seat of a vast and lucrative empire. It permitted its North American colonies far greater economic and political freedom than Spain allowed its dependencies, so the United States entered its independent life with experience of free trade and representative democracy – an enormous advantage in the modern world. The United States also enjoyed an abundant supply of labor, both free and enslaved, while Mexico, severely depleted by a bloody ten-year war for independence, saw its population stagnate throughout most of the nineteenth century.

Mexico's weakness attracted US aggression. When Mexican leaders found that few of their citizens were willing or able to move north to populate the frontier regions that abutted the United States – the territory that is now the US Southwest – they overcame certain misgivings and invited Anglo-Americans from the United States to colonize the territory known as Texas. Most of the colonists who took Mexico up on its offer had no intention of abiding by Mexican law, and Texas soon emerged as a grave problem for the Mexican state. In 1836 the Texans rebelled and claimed their independence. Ten years later, the United States annexed Texas, a move that precipitated the US–Mexican War of 1846–1848. The United States won that war convincingly. According to the terms of the Treaty of Guadalupe Hidalgo, which ended the war, the United States paid Mexico $15 million in exchange for more than half of its territory, including the states of California, Utah, and Nevada, most of Arizona, New Mexico, and Colorado, and a sliver of Wyoming. In 1853, when the United States persuaded Mexico to part with an additional 30,000 square mile chunk of land on it northwest border for a railroad right of way, the border assumed the essential shape it retains to this day: that is, a 2,000-mile-long line that follows the Rio Grande (or Rio Bravo, as it is known to Mexicans) northward and westward from Brownsville, at the southern tip of Texas, to El Paso, then sets out due west through burning deserts and craggy scrubland till it ends in the Pacific Ocean.

The Great Transformation: Mexico

Substantial flows of migrants from Mexico to the United States began with dramatic transformations that took place in both countries in the late nineteenth and early twentieth centuries. In Mexico's case the transformations were wrought by a civil war that brought to power a generation of ambitious folks who subscribed to the ideology of liberalism, and who tried to set Mexico on a firm course toward "modernity." In the process they helped to bring misery and dislocation to vast numbers of their countrymen.

Between 1858 and 1861, Mexicans fought a civil war known as the War of the Reform. In that war, two political persuasions that had been locked in a death match since 1821 had it out once and for all. After two years of the bloodiest fighting Mexico had seen in the four tumultuous decades of its existence, the liberals triumphed decisively over the conservatives. Those liberals thereupon set out to change just about every aspect of Mexican reality. They championed the impartial rule of law; civil liberties, including freedom of religion; free enterprise and free trade; greater social equality; representative government; and compulsory public education. Above all else, the liberals believed in the promise of the individual, and they lamented how the colonial centuries had, in their view, inculcated in the majority of Mexicans a disposition toward dependence and communalism. Much of Mexico's land was owned by the Roman Catholic Church, a corporate entity that, in the liberal view, was an absolute obstacle to the efficiency and profitability that only private enterprise could bring. For the same reason, the liberals decried the communal ownership of land by Indian villages, which had been the tradition since before the conquistadors arrived. They passed a law, known as the Lerdo Law, in 1856, which prohibited the ownership of real estate by "corporations." The church was thus obliged to auction off all of its land except that used in day-to-day operations, and Indian villages were forced to convert their *ejidos* (as communal village lands were called) into individually owned plots. The liberals hoped in this manner to make agriculture a fully commercial enterprise that would enlarge the food supply, provide goods for foreign exchange, and increase revenues accruing to the state, all of which would underwrite a transition to industrialism and modernity. For a variety of reasons, the law's results were disappointing to say the least, but it is undeniable that it brought about a major change in the Mexican countryside, one that brought capitalism to rural Mexico – capitalism of the most rapacious and unforgiving kind.

The leader who sent these changes into high gear was General Porfirio Díaz, who seized power in a military rebellion in 1876. Although his rebellion was guided by the slogan "Effective suffrage and no reelection," Díaz went on to hold sway as Mexico's dictator for the next 35 years. Once in power, he adopted a new slogan: "Order and Progress." This slogan was inspired by a philosophy known as Positivism, which was championed by the French thinker Auguste Comte. "Order," for those who subscribed to Positivism, meant an end to democratic politics, which Mexico's history tended to suggest were inevitably disorderly and divisive. The leading architects of the Porfirian system styled themselves *científicos* – not scientists, exactly, but "men of science." They believed that governing should be done by experts, men who knew what was best for society – what, that is, would best ensure "progress" – and who would not have to answer to "the people." Porfirio Díaz, for them, was the necessary man of his time, a man who enjoyed nearly universal admiration (at least for a while) and who had the skills to keep the nation from descending into anarchy.

The second part of the *científicos'* formula – "progress" – meant an ambitious program of commercializing Mexican agriculture to make it productive and profitable in the hope it would underwrite the development of industry. The problem lay in the fact that Mexico, in the late nineteenth century, was a poor country, with relatively few well-heeled entrepreneurs willing and able to invest in the target areas: building railroads, founding banks, revitalizing ports, pioneering new crops, exploring for new minerals, drilling for oil, and building new factories. Such capital, the *científicos* reasoned, would have to be imported from abroad, and it would have to be wooed to Mexico with generous concessions – tax breaks, rights of way, land grants, and cheap labor.

To ensure the latter enticement – cheap labor – the Díaz government outlawed labor unions and gave employers carte blanche to behave as callously as they wished. Repression of labor during the Porfiriato – as the period of Díaz's dictatorship is known – was notorious. One of the more famous accounts, journalist John Kenneth Turner's aptly titled *Barbarous Mexico*, contains harrowing descriptions of Maya and Yaqui Indians forced to work as slaves on hemp plantations under the brutal sun of Yucatán, starting well before daylight and ending well after sunset, their day's only meal a couple of tortillas, a cup of beans, and a bowl of rancid fish broth; and of people shanghaied by local political bosses or corrupt labor contractors to work on the tobacco plantations of the Valle Nacional in Oaxaca, where overwork, lack of food, and exposure to disease guaranteed certain death within a space of seven or eight months. Similarly horrifying conditions prevailed on rubber, fruit, coffee, and sugar plantations, as well as in the tropical hardwood industry. Most of the producers who used such virtual slave labor raised goods for export. Most Mexicans were poor, barely able to afford corn and beans and some sort of roof over their heads; they consumed very little. Economic production, then, was a show put on largely for a foreign – mostly American – audience. American capitalists found the lure of so much cheap labor well-nigh irresistible. Ex-president Ulysses S. Grant, toward the end of his life, took to preaching the boundless opportunities for American capital in Mexico, mostly because, in addition to many valuable natural resources, Mexico could furnish workers who were "industrious, frugal, and willing to work for a pittance, if afforded an opportunity."[1]

Little is known about Mexicans who migrated to the United States prior to 1910. Most of those who crossed the border were likely itinerant workers – ranch hands, mine workers, railroad workers, and the like. Rural folk in the region that eventually emerged as the overwhelming source of migrants – the north-central states of Michoacán, Jalisco, Guanajuato, San Luis Potosí, Zacatecas, and Durango – were reasonably well off, at least by the harsh standards of Porfirian Mexico. Most were permanent employees of *haciendas* (as large farms were called) who received guaranteed monthly wages, rations of corn to meet their family's needs, grazing and planting rights, and free, if humble, housing. Others were temporary workers, who lacked the security of the permanent workforce, but were somewhat compensated by being paid higher wages. This is not to say conditions were enviable. The people of the center -north suffered along with the rest of the Mexican people as the population expanded rapidly even while wages stagnated and the price of basic foodstuffs rose. But this was not enough of a "push" to send people trekking toward the border in large numbers. Something more would have to happen before that exodus began. A large part of that "something" was the advent of railroads.

The development of railroads linking Mexico to the United States was perhaps inevitable, but it took some time. When Porfirio Díaz first came to power, the US–Mexican border was a source of considerable international tension, for it was largely the domain of criminals, smugglers, hostile Indians, and US troops demanding to be allowed to use whatever means necessary to calm the situation. And any leader of Mexico hoping to consolidate a base of support had to rattle a few sabers in the direction of the United States. So Díaz, shortly after seizing power, canceled a railroad concession that his predecessor had granted to an American firm. A year later, Díaz's Development Minister negotiated a contract with another American company to build a railroad connecting Mexico City to the US border, with a branch to the Pacific at either San Blas or Manzanillo, but the Mexican Congress overruled it, wanting no part of a rail connection to the Northern Colossus. Alfredo Chávez, a leading voice in Congress on the matter, explained the reasoning: "Nations of the North generally invade nations of the South," therefore "we should always fear the United States."[2]

The construction of roads to facilitate trade with Mexico had been a goal of the United States ever since its first Minister to Mexico, Joel Poinsett, had tried without success to interest the Mexicans in cooperating on a highway connecting Mexico City to Santa Fe and St. Louis. In April 1877 the United States granted its official recognition to the Díaz regime. A year later, US Minister to Mexico John W. Foster made a high-profile case that trade would be a boon to both countries, but that at present it was obstructed by the "revolutionary character of the country, the want of protection to American citizens and capital, and the opposition to railroad connections to the United States."[3] The time seemed ripe for railroad building, since many diplomatic problems had been smoothed over and Díaz had adopted a more conciliatory attitude. Although Mexican officials remained leery of US domination of railroad lines, they did not have sufficient capital to carry out such projects themselves. They also shared American enthusiasm for increased trade. Accordingly, the first American railroad to be built in Mexico was incorporated in Boston under the laws of Massachusetts. With a generous concession and subsidies from the Mexican government, that railroad – completed in 1884 – connected Mexico City to Ciudad Juárez/El Paso, where it went on to link to the Southern Pacific Railroad. Soon enough, branch lines and competing railroads connected nearly every major city and zone of production in Mexico to nearly every major city in the United States. When Díaz came to power in 1876, Mexico had only 416 miles of railroad track; when he left in 1911, Mexico had 15,360 miles of track, and United States companies and United States capital had built some 70 percent of it.

The changes that came about in Mexico during the Porfiriato are important to the story of Mexican migration to the United States for several reasons. First, they created social, economic, and political tensions that, in 1910, would explode in an epic bloodletting known as the Mexican Revolution, and that horrific violence provided a major motivation to migrants. Second, the architects of Porfirian development sought quite deliberately to court foreign – mostly, but not exclusively, American – capital with the enticement of cheap labor, generous concessions, and lax regulation. Once established, that pattern proved devilishly resistant to change. Third, and finally, the completion of an international rail system was crucial to the immigration story for several reasons: it made it far easier and cheaper to travel to the northern border from anywhere in Mexico; it facilitated an increase in trade, which meant a growing commercialization of agriculture, which in turn meant a rise in land values and the dispossession of poor rural landowners; and it led to a sharp increase in communication and trade, which effectively made Mexico an economic satellite of the United States. By the early 1890s the United States was buying 70 percent of Mexico's exports, while Mexico bought 56 percent of its imports from the United States. US corporations came to own nearly all of Mexico's mineral and oil deposits, vast quantities of choice Mexican farm and pastoral lands, and some key industries. Mexico also came to be linked so closely to the US economy that a recession in the United States was often felt as a depression in Mexico. As the Mexican population continued to grow, while economic opportunities remained stagnant, the ranks of the Mexican poor exploded. Migration to the north was now both feasible and, increasingly, necessary.

The Great Transformation: The Southwestern United States

These changes in Mexico followed or coincided with momentous changes in the United States. There, railroad building had been going on for some time. The first transcontinental railway was completed in 1869 with the joining of the Central Pacific and Union Pacific Railways at Promontory Summit, Utah. Once completed, the Southern Pacific Railroad garnered immense power, dominating western land and politics and employing all manner of corrupt and abusive practices, including, essentially, donating public lands to itself.

During the late eighteenth century, the West was very sparsely populated, so labor for mines and railroad crews consisted almost entirely of immigrants. Railroad companies maintained the curious practice of determining wages according to the worker's nationality or ethnic group, with Mexicans the lowest paid of all. The heyday of western railroad building coincided with a steadily increasing popular and official hostility toward Asians, who had made up a large majority of workers on the Central Pacific line. Chinese, who commonly worked as shopkeepers, common laborers, launderers, and fruit pickers, made convenient scapegoats whenever the economy of the southwestern states suffered a downturn. Organized labor, small manufacturers, and small farmers claimed that the willingness of the Chinese to work for meager wages depressed the economy and gave unfair advantages to the big farmers and manufacturers who were crowding out the little guys. Chinese were murdered with impunity, and they were the targets of discriminatory legislation. The California constitution of 1879 charged that the Chinese were, or were likely to become, "vagrants, paupers, mendicants, criminals, or invalids afflicted with contagious or infectious diseases," and in order to protect the "well-being of the state" it forbade corporations to hire them, barred them from working on public works projects, and permitted cities and towns to expel them or herd them in ghettoes. In 1882 the federal government passed the Chinese Exclusion Act, which effectively cut off further immigration from China.

Hostility also focused on the Japanese, who tended to be more successful in acquiring land of their own and who formed clan-based mutual aid societies to aid their agricultural operations. California landowners did not welcome the competition. At the national level, the United States and Japan worked out a so-called "Gentlemen's Agreement" in 1907, which virtually ended Japanese migration to the United States. For good measure, California land barons pushed for the passage of an Alien Land Law, which went into force in 1913, barring persons ineligible for citizenship – namely, Asians – from owning real estate. Migrants from southern and eastern Europe also faced growing discrimination in a nativist movement – that is, a movement that sought to privilege citizens over immigrants – that eventually culminated in the Immigration Act of 1924, which made a large portion of the world's people officially unwelcome in the United States.

All of this left employers the choice of either paying higher wages in an effort to attract citizen laborers, or recruiting Mexicans. Of course, they chose to recruit Mexicans, who by 1900 made up between 70 and 90 percent of the track crews on the railroads of the Southwest. To recruit Mexicans, southwestern employers built up an ambitious recruiting system, with contracting offices in US border towns, and Mexican recruiters enticing workers deep in the Mexican interior with promises of jobs and riches to be gained in the United States. The US immigration law of 1885 explicitly outlawed luring workers in foreign countries with promises of work – this seemed too much like indentured servitude, something that legislators decided was un-American – but employers ignored the provision against contract labor and the authorities did not enforce it. Recruitment proved easy enough: farm laborers in Mexico were paid between 12 and 15 cents a day, whereas railroad workers in the United States earned about a dollar a day. And from there it got even better: other industries found it easy to lure away the Mexican workers that the railroads had recruited, since work in mines and smelters paid $2.46 a day. Mexicans quickly came to dominate the labor force in the copper mines near the border.

In contrast to the case of the Asians, there was little popular hostility toward Mexicans. That was not due primarily to racial tolerance on the part of the Americans, but rather to the fact that Mexicans in the United States were still relatively few in number and they tended to work in mines or on railroad lines, well away from population centers. If complaints about their presence should arise, employers burnished their stock retort, namely, that, unlike the Asians, if Mexicans should ever prove objectionable, sending them home would be comparatively cheap and easy.

By 1900, tracks linked most of the major cities of the West and Middle West to the populous East, making possible the shipment of goods to lucrative eastern markets. But, as of 1900, the arid and sparsely populated West had few goods to ship. Cotton was farmed commercially in east Texas, and in California wheat was grown extensively, mostly for local consumption. But the Southwest was still far from the agricultural powerhouse it would become. That began to change in 1902 when the US Congress passed the National Reclamation Act – also known as the Newlands Act, in honor of its author, Representative Francis G. Newlands of Nevada – which made available the proceeds of public land sales in the West and Southwest to build and maintain large-scale irrigation works. Soon, the Great American Desert began to disappear, replaced by an agricultural oasis that yielded vast quantities of cotton, vegetables, fruits, and grains. At the same time, the advent of refrigerated railroad cars and new techniques for drying and canning produce made it feasible to ship perishable products over vast distances, to markets in the Midwest and East.

The transformation was rapid and impressive. In 1900 the southwestern states accounted for practically none of the produce sold in the markets of the Midwest and East; by 1929 those states accounted for about 40 percent of that produce. The amount of irrigated land in California increased by more than 2 million acres between 1909 and 1929, while Texas saw a 317 percent increase. Cotton cultivation spread from east Texas into south, central, and west Texas, and later huge cotton plantations appeared in the Mesilla Valley of New Mexico and in the Imperial and San Joaquin Valleys of California – places where temperatures routinely hit between 100 and 112 degrees Fahrenheit, and where willing workers were hard to come by.

As formerly desolate lands began rendering tons of produce, the value of those lands skyrocketed. In California an acre of land that sold for around $25 in 1900 was fetching $115 by 1925. Meanwhile, new technologies such as steam shovels, dynamite, and improved surveying instruments led to a boom in copper and coal mining in New Mexico, Arizona, Oklahoma, and Colorado. New employment opportunities also emerged in midwestern industries, including meatpacking plants, steel mills, textile mills, and railroad maintenance. Yet the population of these regions remained sparse, and the federal government insisted on making it sparser still with its prohibitions against immigration from Asia and increasing harassment of Europeans who made up a significant part of the workforce. That left the Mexicans, who became the region's established working class. And Mexicans proved to be a big hit with southwestern farmers. A 1907 edition of the magazine *California Fruit Grower* described them as "plentiful, generally peaceable, and ... satisfied with very low social conditions."[4] These were traits that southwestern growers greatly admired.

California's agricultural development deserves a bit of special attention, given that that state's farms acquired a well-nigh insatiable appetite for transitory labor, and so it became the destination for the largest numbers of Mexican immigrants. Critics found in California the most egregious case of the evils of capitalism imaginable. Famed reformer Henry George, writing in 1871, described the apportioning of land in

California as "a history of greed, of perjury, of corruption, of spoliation and high-handed robbery, for which it will be difficult to find a parallel," while Karl Marx allowed that "nowhere else has the upheaval most shamelessly caused by capitalist centralization taken place with such speed."[5]

No sooner had California been acquired by the United States at the close of the US–Mexican War than a distinctive pattern of land ownership emerged. As long as it owned California, Mexico had maintained the policy of making very generous grants of land to anyone who was willing to pick up stakes and settle in that remote territory, something few Mexicans were inclined to do. The policy made sense considering that Mexico's objective was to attract people to its northern frontier region with generous enticements. But, on the eve of the US–Mexican War, schemers and speculators scrambled to secure enormous land grants, and the recipients of such grants were able to make certain that the Treaty of Guadalupe Hidalgo, which ended the war, ensured their grants would be recognized as valid. So an enormous swath of California's land was carved up among a handful of people even before California was admitted to the American union in 1850. One commonly used tactic was for a grant holder to wait till settlers had moved in and improved a piece of land, whereupon he would produce his claim and appeal to the courts to have the settlers evicted. The courts, partners in such rascality, nearly always obliged.

Other methods were used to solidify the monopolization of land by a few wealthy people. Well-connected individuals were able to buy so-called "swamplands" that had been given to the state by the federal government, paying only a nominal fee. One of California's greatest early landowners once had himself pulled around his land in a boat hitched to a team of horses so that he could righteously declare that it was indeed "swampland." By 1870 one five hundredth of the state's population owned half of the state's farmland, and those folks were, of course, well positioned when land values increased after 1900. According to Henry George, some of those estates were so vast that "a strong horse cannot gallop [across them] in a day, and one may travel for miles and miles over fertile ground where no plow has ever struck, but which is all owned, and on which no settler can come to make himself a home, unless he pay such tribute as the lord of the domain choose to exact."[6]

Aspiring homesteaders arriving in California were out of luck. Many of those who received no land, or who were forced off of land they thought was their own, became tenant farmers or joined a burgeoning army of migrant workers, soon a fixture on the California landscape. Variously called tramps, hoboes, or bindle-stiffs, these men would work for a season and then move on to the next crop, the next harvest, putting down no roots and all the while remaining desperately poor. Like the immigrant workers who came later, they were creatures of capitalism, California-style.

The railroads, too, were able to secure immense land grants – some 20 million acres by 1870. They engaged in the same sort of shenanigans that so many private landowners had used. Settlers would move in, occupy and improve a parcel of land that they imagined to be their own, only to find that the land in question was in fact a bit of unsurveyed right-of-way claimed by the railroad. The settlers would be evicted, and the railroad would take over the land, improvements and all. In fact, the railroads actually encouraged settlement for the very purpose of appropriating already-improved land. The Southern Pacific Railroad had the support of the state government because, in many ways, it *was* the state government. The Southern Pacific was instrumental in deciding who got what land and under what terms, and it ensured that the great landed estates of California remained essentially untaxed. Occasional murmurs of dissent were silenced, at times with great brutality.

The attitude that took hold among the great landowners of California was a reckless one. They were not much interested in diversifying their crops or using scientific methods, nor did they let their fields lie fallow or use fertilizers. The soils were quickly exhausted, leading to a pattern of adopting and then abandoning crops in succession. Wheat was the main crop until 1870, when it became unprofitable and was replaced by fruits. In 1897 a new, very stiff tariff against imported sugar was passed by the US Congress, leading to a huge boom in the cultivation of sugar beets throughout the Southwest. In 1902 California sugar beet farmers merged their enterprises into the Sugar Trust, enabling them to set the price of sugar beets and drive small farmers out of business. The Sugar Trust ensured that the sugar beet industry, like so much of California's agriculture, was concentrated in very few hands.

Activist-journalist Carey McWilliams, writing in the late 1930s, noted that travelers in California – the nation's premiere farm state – would see few of the trappings that they might associate with rural life. Lacking were "the schoolhouse on the hilltop, the comfortable homes, the compact and easy indolence of the countryside. Where are the farms? Where are the farmhouses?"[7] Instead, travelers would see vast, intensive, mechanized operations, "factories in the field." Crucial to these factories was an itinerant rural proletariat. And since the development of this pattern of land holding and land use coincided with a major backlash against Asian immigrants, and since relatively few Americans, white or black, would willingly give up the comforts of home for an endlessly monotonous, endlessly oppressive and impoverished life on the road, that meant that the hard work of California agriculture came to be done almost entirely by Mexicans.

The Mexican Revolution

Mexico's history prior to 1876 was one of almost ceaseless upheaval – popular uprisings, political rebellions, foreign interventions, and civil wars. The Díaz dictatorship, while punctuated by periodic violence, brought about an era often referred to as the "Pax Porfiriana," for there were no major tumults during those 34 years (1876–1910). But the ingredients for upheaval were gathered during the Porfiriato, and the recipe was unwittingly concocted: a combination of popular rage at poverty, marginalization, and general lack of fairness; nationalist resentment of Díaz's favoritism toward foreigners at the expense of Mexicans; discontent in some circles – most notably the army – at Díaz's inability to keep from growing old, and his refusal to take matters of political succession seriously, which threatened an ugly power struggle in the offing; and a stifling system of favoritism, political cronyism, and autocracy that allowed few opportunities for the small but growing middle class.

In 1910 Díaz's power was challenged by a diminutive, wealthy landowner from northern Mexico named Francisco I. Madero. Madero attracted deliriously enthusiastic crowds wherever he campaigned, and his movement grew steadily, even despite repression unleashed by the authorities. When it became clear that Díaz had no intention of allowing a free and fair election, Madero went to San Antonio, Texas, and plotted violent revolution. It soon became apparent that Madero's chief problem – which he seems not to have completely understood – was that building a viable coalition of people who had such disparate and irreconcilable complaints was impossible. Madero's movement was probably doomed from the start.

The revolution broke out in November 1910, and its first phase ended in May 1911 with Díaz's resignation. Madero was elected in November 1911, but long before that happened serious dissension had erupted in Mexico, and that dissension led to Madero's overthrow and assassination in February 1913. From that point, Mexico descended into unremitting violence and chaos, which did not seriously begin to abate until after 1917.

The years of revolution mark the start of substantial migration from Mexico to the United States. The revolution gave Mexicans plenty of reason to flee their country: horrific violence, epidemic disease, starvation, and runaway inflation. Agriculture practically ground to a halt as the armies of several revolutionary factions, joined by marauders and brigands, occupied abandoned haciendas, looting and pillaging and destroying all along their way. The price of corn rose tenfold, and real wages dropped by three quarters between 1913 and 1916, the years of greatest violence. Revolutionary violence was especially intense in those states that were fast emerging as the prime "sending states," especially the center-north states of Michoacán, Jalisco, San Luis Potosí, Zacatecas, Durango, and Guanajuato. Although the people of that region tended to be fairly passive toward the struggle, the revolution followed the railroads. And, since the center-north was between central Mexico and northern border, railroads crisscrossed it like a spider's web, ensuring that the destruction was especially intense there. Agriculture in that region, which before the revolution was among the most productive in the country, was virtually destroyed.

Terrifying though it was, the violence and hardship of the revolution were not necessarily the definitive factors in provoking massive migration. They certainly provided an important "push," but only when the push was joined by the "pull" of available, relatively high-paying jobs in the United States did migration really pick up. The volume of

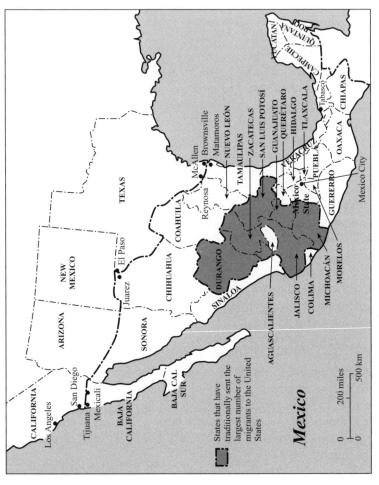

Figure 1.1 Map of Mexico and the sending region.

immigration from Mexico began to rise in earnest in 1918, just as the violence in Mexico was winding down. In that year, the United States entered into World War I. About a million US citizens were conscripted into the military, while at the same time impoverished whites and blacks went north to take relatively high-paying factory jobs, creating a severe shortage of labor that Mexicans were invited to fill. According to estimates – which are necessarily unreliable, since keeping close track of thousands of transients is virtually impossible – fewer than 50,000 Mexicans migrated to the United States in the first decade of the twentieth century; the second decade witnessed the migration of some 219,004; and the third (1921–1930) more than doubled that number, to 459,259.

Even so, the importance of the Mexican Revolution with respect of immigration would be hard to overstate, for its impact went well beyond the hideous violence of its epic phase. It was especially important for the character of the regimes it brought to power and the kinds of reforms they championed. In 1920, as the revolution's most violent phase came to an end, power was seized by a triumvirate of men who hailed from the northwestern border state of Sonora. The most important of these, Generals Alvaro Obregón and Plutarco Elías Calles, who ruled Mexico formally or from behind the scenes from 1920 to 1934, styled themselves champions of the downtrodden, the victors in a massive popular uprising whose most fundamental demand was social justice. A new Constitution, promulgated in 1917, contained one of the most progressive labor laws in the world for its time. That Constitution mandated eight hour workdays and six day work weeks; a minimum wage; equal pay for equal work regardless of race, gender, or nationality; an end to child labor; and the right to strike and bargain collectively. In the ensuing decades those provisions were often honored in the breach.

Obregón and Calles largely based their power on a close alliance with the industrial working class, as presented by a moderate labor union called the Regional Confederation of Mexican Workers (or CROM, in its Spanish acronym). But the industrial working class was still a small sector of the Mexican workforce. The Mexican Revolution was largely a rural phenomenon, with much of its violence fueled by peasant anger. The epicenter of the rural revolt was the state of Morelos, where peasants had been illegally deprived of their lands by politically connected sugar barons, for the most part absentee landlords collecting the profits from vast sugar plantations. The peasants of Morelos were joined by other rural folk, mostly from the south-central part of the country, whose grievances were deep but varied.

This was a world that the Sonoran generals, who led the country after the revolution, did not understand very well. They knew, however, that the demand for "land and liberty" – the slogan of the followers of the leading agrarian rebel, Emiliano Zapata – would need to be placated. The land reform provisions that were incorporated into the 1917 Constitution were quite radical. Villages desiring land grants did not have to prove that their lands had been illegally taken from them, but only that they lacked sufficient lands to meet the needs of the village population, as determined by government agents. Once it had been certified as needy, a village could formally petition for lands, which were to be taken from surrounding haciendas and granted in the form of *ejidos*. The *ejido* was an extent of land that was farmed by a village communally. It was an old colonial-era institution that had been done away with by the liberal reformers of mid-century, who believed strongly in the redemptive power of individual private property. *Ejido* lands were technically owned by the state, and they were administered by village *ejidal* committees, who would decide who could farm which parcel and, in conjunction with higher-level institutions, what to grow and how to market what was grown. The land could not be bought, sold, used as collateral for loans, or alienated in any way.

The *ejido* was, in fact, an ambiguous concept, and the revolutionary elite responsible for carrying out the agrarian reform could not agree on what exactly it meant or how it should operate. Obregón and Calles made it fairly clear that they had little use for the *ejido*, and carried out a halting agrarian reform mostly as a matter of political expediency. By the late 1920s, the Calles government was drastically scaling back the pace of land distribution.

The center-north region, which was fast emerging as the primary sender of migrants to the United States, benefited little from revolutionary reforms. The destruction of the revolution was compounded by a severe drought in 1917. By that time, agriculture had ground to a halt on all of the large haciendas of the region, leaving rural people – most of whom had been attached to the haciendas either as resident workers or as day laborers – without employment. Meanwhile, the price of corn was ten to fifteen times what it had been in 1910, and buying power – for those lucky enough to have some income – declined by 75 percent. Epidemic disease added to the misery, especially the great Spanish influenza of 1918, which viciously attacked this weakened social organism. Some people reverted to the primitive, hunting small game or gathering edible weeds and herbs. Others moved to the cities in hopes of finding work, while many others headed north to take advantage of the wartime boom in the United States.

Even when peace returned to the center-north region, landowners had little capital to spend, and they were in any case loathe to spend what they had in a climate of such uncertainty, where their lands might at any time be invaded by squatters or seized by the government. In fact, the common folk of the region were mortally skeptical of the Mexican government, and few of them applied for land grants. Most people, once agricultural operations resumed after 1920, became sharecroppers or tenants, assuming the risks and burdens that had previously belonged almost exclusively to the landowners. Prices remained very high, and conditions were worsened by a sudden spurt in population growth.

Then, in 1926, came yet another blow: President Plutarco Elías Calles decided to enforce some provisions of the 1917 Constitution that entailed the persecution of the Catholic clergy. The result was a bloody rebellion known as the Cristero War, owing to the rebels' war cry, "*¡Viva Cristo Rey!*" ("Long Live Christ the King!"). The Cristero War was particularly fierce in the conservative, religious, government-hating region of the center-north – precisely those states that were already undergoing such great trials. The Cristero War cost roughly 90,000 lives and forced many people into exile. It also added further to the ongoing plunge in food production. The Mexican government sought to punish landowners who had given aid and comfort to the Cristero rebels by seizing and dividing their haciendas into *ejidos*, even if the recipients balked at such largess. Mexico was forced to spend millions importing corn and beans merely to meet the most basic nutritional needs of the population, but the imports barely kept pace with population growth, and the specter of starvation remained very real to many Mexicans.

In the mid-1920s a team of Mexican anthropologists ran some calculations and arrived at some shocking conclusions. They listed the prices in Mexico of many articles of primary necessity – food, fuel, clothing, and shelter. They determined that subsistence in Mexico at the most marginal level – excluding expenses for such luxuries as education and recreation – would cost approximately US$144 per month. The average rural worker in Mexico earned less than $18 a month. A factory worker, meanwhile, earned a little over $60 a month. So a rural worker's wages would have had to increase more than eightfold, and a factory worker's wage would have had to more than double, merely to afford the barest essentials of life. Low as they were, wages paid to unskilled workers in the United States were very attractive to people suffering privation on such a scale. Unfortunately, the huge discrepancy in wages was a two-edged sword, for it allowed US employers accused of abusing their Mexican workers to say, not without some justice, that conditions in the United States at their worst were probably better than conditions in Mexico.[8]

Within Mexico, there was much ambivalence toward the migration issue. Many educated Mexicans viewed emigration as a national disgrace, a humiliating sign that Mexico could not meet the needs of its own citizens. Some went so far as to vent against the migrants themselves, portraying them as traitors who peddled their labor abroad rather than stay and work where they were needed. They fretted that perhaps those migrants would be swayed by Protestant missionaries, or would adopt the notoriously libertine practices of the neighboring republic. Others – notably, anthropologist Manuel Gamio – had a more optimistic view, comparing time spent in the United States to attending a "giant university" where Mexicans could gain "valuable experience in agriculture or industry," learn to "handle machinery and modern tools," acquire "discipline and steady habits of work," and improve their material culture, returning better dressed, better nourished, more literate, more frugal, more ambitious, and less fanatically religious.[9]

The Mexican government, in its various manifestations over the years, was also ambivalent. It billed itself as a government that arose from a quintessentially popular revolution, and as such the legitimate representative of the peasants and workers who made the revolution. The apparent fact that this revolutionary government could not provide adequate employment for those same peasants and workers was a major embarrassment that some regimes tried to compensate for by insisting that their nationals abroad be scrupulously well treated.

Most Mexican leaders overcame their embarrassment for eminently practical reasons, which have remained salient down to the present day. Migrants sent large quantities of money to their families back home – so much that such remittances became a key source of foreign exchange for Mexico. Moreover, Mexican governments greatly appreciated the so -called "safety-valve" effect. Many of those who left for the United States were among Mexico's poorest, yet the very fact that they had the gumption to migrate suggested that they were ambitious and enterprising. They were, government officials reasoned, the very type that might, if kept home, become mired in frustration, adopt rebellious attitudes, and cause serious domestic strife. And every person who left was one fewer person who needed to be provided with a job in Mexico, where jobs were perilously scarce.

The United States, ca. 1910–1930: Xenophobia and Employment

Prior to 1917 the only obstacles for Mexicans wishing to enter the United States were the expense of the voyage and the forbidding terrain. No laws barred their entry into the United States, and only about sixty Bureau of Immigration agents patrolled the 2,000 miles of border.

During the nineteenth century, nationalism – that is, a deep and sometimes belligerent devotion to the nation and its supposed interests – had become a potent and destabilizing force in the world. Nationalism reached something of a crescendo in World War I, which was largely a bloody outburst of bellicose chauvinism among the nations of Europe. For the first time, nations began issuing passports to regulate international migration. The United States was no exception: as it ramped up for its entry into the Great War, nationalism reared its head, as did nationalism's first cousin, xenophobia. There arose a veritable mania for protecting the nation's territorial and racial integrity, which meant that national minorities and immigrants came increasingly to be seen as treacherous organisms that threatened to infect the national bloodstream. Of course, since Germany was the enemy in the Great War,

Germans and German Americans were singled out for the harshest treatment. But peoples of southern and eastern Europe were also targeted, since they were more likely to be Catholics or Jews who, in the official racial ideology of the day, were considered not only to be racially inferior to whites descended from "Nordic" stock, but especially susceptible to anarchist and Bolshevik propaganda.

The Immigration Act of 1917 was an expression of these growing sentiments. Ostensibly, it was aimed at persons who were "likely to become public charges" – an ample category that included, among others, drunks, beggars, epileptics, anarchists, the "feeble-minded," and the insane. In fact, the Act's racist undertones were unmistakable. It broadened discrimination against Asians by creating an "Asiatic Barred Zone," which proscribed all immigration from a region extending from Afghanistan to the Pacific. Now it was not just the Chinese and Japanese who were unwelcome, but all other Asians as well. The law also forced would-be immigrants to pass a reading test in at least one language, imposed an $8 head tax for immigrants upon entering the United States, and declared it illegal to immigrate in response to promises of work, whether or not such promises were true. Southwestern growers howled in protest, for the law, as intended, quickly brought about a decrease of nearly 50 percent in immigration of workers from Italy, Greece, Portugal, and the Slavic countries of eastern Europe – hitherto a significant part of their workforce. Meanwhile, since roughly three quarters of Mexicans – and nearly all Mexican immigrants – were illiterate, and since $8 was a considerable sum for impoverished Mexicans, employers fretted that their only remaining option for labor was imperiled.

Making matters especially dicey, the new immigration restrictions were promulgated at a time of unprecedented expansion in southwestern agriculture, since World War I generated enormous demand for food and agricultural raw materials. The growers were able to paint a harrowing picture of what would happen if heroic remedies were not implemented: agriculture collapsing, fertile lands reverting to howling desert, the war effort and US security endangered. They had much support at a time when popular magazines and newsreels routinely proclaimed that "Food Will Win the War." And they prevailed, pushing through a proviso in the law that allowed the Secretary of Labor to set aside the law's provisions if, upon investigation, he became convinced that a labor shortage was imminent in any given sector of the economy. On May 23, 1917, Secretary of Labor William B. Wilson specifically exempted temporary workers from Mexico from the provisions of the 1917 Act, and in the summer of 1918 he extended this waiver to Mexicans working in construction, mining, railroads, and factories. This was the start of what is sometimes called the first "*bracero* program." (*Bracero*, a term derived from the Spanish word *brazo*, or "arm," commonly refers to an unskilled, usually agricultural, laborer.) Secretary Wilson began a government directed effort to help growers and other employers meet their labor needs in this emergency situation.

About a quarter of a million Mexicans entered the United States under the terms of the waiver between 1918 and 1920. Employers were pleased with the initiative generally, but less than delighted by the red tape that, they felt, gummed up the works. Employers had the burden of proving they had a genuine need for labor; workers were to be provided with picture identification cards upon entering the United States; contracts were limited to six months; and employers were enjoined to withhold 25 cents a day from each worker's wages to ensure that the worker would have the wherewithal to return to Mexico once his contract expired. Employers complained that such regulations would discourage immigration, which was the last thing they wanted to see. Their chief advocate in government, Food Administrator Herbert Hoover, made their case for them. Hoover was especially critical of the policy of limiting workers' stays to six months, and of compelling employers to withhold funds to ensure their workers' return to Mexico. Hoover and his constituents did not want the Mexicans to go home, but to continue working for low wages as long as their bodies held out. If there were no withholding, he seems to have reasoned, those immigrants would be too poor to go home.

To be sure, many Mexicans who had no patience for the bureaucratic snags could simply enter the country illegally, and many of them did so. It was during these same years that a couple of new and enduring characters made their first appearance on the scene: the undocumented immigrant, popularly known as the "wetback" (*mojado* in Spanish) because many swam the Rio Grande to enter the United States (prior to 1917, there were no illegal Mexican immigrants for the obvious reason that there were no laws restricting Mexican immigration); and the *coyote*, a professional people smuggler who, for a fee, helped to ensure the immigrant a successful entry. By 1920 the flow of migrants over the border was becoming torrential. There were a couple of episodes that slowed that flow, but only briefly. In the spring and summer of 1917 a rumor ran through the Mexican migrant community that Mexicans were going to be drafted into the US Army. Where these rumors started is not known, but some US consuls insisted they were deliberately spread by German agents or German sympathizers hoping to sabotage the US war effort. If so, the ploy nearly worked, because suddenly hundreds of panicked immigrants were fleeing back across the southern border. There were, in fact, a few cases of Mexicans mistakenly or illegally drafted into the US military, but it was never a matter of policy. The mass exodus of Mexican workers under the conditions that prevailed in the summer of 1917 could be disastrous, since it would affect both agricultural production and rail transport of vital military supplies. US officials, accordingly, enlisted Mexican consuls, newspaper editors, Roman Catholic clerics, the military, and US citizens to help them persuade Mexican workers that the rumors were unfounded. Spanish language posters appeared in many a Texas town assuring that no Mexicans were to be drafted. By late summer of 1917 the exodus had slowed considerably, but the campaign to override the rumor went on well into 1918.

A second circumstance briefly interrupted the flow of labor over the border. In early 1921 the wartime economic boom played out suddenly, and the US economy entered into a grave, if short-lived, crisis. Some 5 million people were thrown out of work, 100,000 businesses went bankrupt, and nearly half a million farmers lost their land. Mexican workers were among the poorest and most expendable elements in the US labor market, so the depression hit them especially hard. Local charities that tried to provide relief soon found themselves swamped. They implored the US Congress to allocate a special fund to deport the Mexicans back to Mexico, but Congress paid no heed to their requests. Some desperate Mexicans moved to cities in the hope of finding work, often ending up homeless and still more desperate. Meanwhile, the companies that employed Mexican laborers put their cynicism and hypocrisy on full display, and not for the last time. They had been unstinting in their praise for Mexican workers during times when there was a shortage of labor and their profits were threatened, though they considered the Mexicans' most admirable trait that they were willing to work hard for very little money and without complaint. Those employers were directly responsible for the Mexicans' presence in the United States – they had actively enticed Mexicans to cross the border and expended tremendous effort to ensure that government regulations that might have impeded their crossing be waived – but now they refused to take any responsibility for helping the Mexicans return home. After the economy rebounded, they once again boisterously sang the praises of the noble Mexican worker. Meanwhile, Mexicans in some locales made handy scapegoats for the economic hard times. In Ft. Worth, Texas, Mexicans were threatened with mass murder; dozens of unemployed and homeless Mexicans in Denver, Colorado, were arrested for vagrancy and put to work on chain gangs; and in Ranger, Texas, masked Ku Klux Klan night riders raided an ad hoc Mexican labor camp, dragging about a hundred men, women, and children from the tents and beating them.

The Mexican government involved itself fairly extensively with the migrant community for the first time. Even though Mexico's economy was in an even more deplorable condition than that of the United States, the government spent over a million dollars to feed immigrants and transport them home. The expenditures had an impact, though a relatively small one: the Mexican government aided roughly 50,000 Mexicans, out of a population that is impossible to estimate, but was presumed to number between 260,000 and 1 million.

By 1923 the US economy had rebounded, and the welcome mat was once again rolled out for Mexicans.

2

Restriction, Depression, and Deportation
The 1920s and 1930s

In the United States the first couple of decades of the twentieth century witnessed a rising tide of nationalism and xenophobia. The most prominent targets of that building hatred were Asians and eastern Europeans, though Mexican immigration reached sufficient volume by the 1920s that Mexicans were awarded a place of honor on the unwanted list. Still, the debate that erupted about how to deal with Mexicans was complicated by a number of factors, including perpetual cries of labor shortages from employers in the southwestern United States and America's gradually shifting policies toward Latin America. Thanks to those complications, there were few restrictions on Mexican immigration prior to 1929, even while immigration by other nationalities was greatly restricted during the 1910s and 1920s. With the start of the Great Depression in 1929, Mexicans emerged as favorite scapegoats, and were deported from the country en masse. But some who remained took part in some courageous, if ultimately futile, labor actions, demonstrating that the trait employers claimed most to admire about Mexicans – namely, their supposed docility and lack of ambition – was badly exaggerated.

Beyond Borders: A History of Mexican Migration to the United States
By Timothy J. Henderson
© 2011 Timothy J. Henderson

The Restriction Debate and the Immigration Act of 1924

During the first two decades of the twentieth century, even though Mexican immigration to the United States was substantial, there was no popular xenophobic outcry aimed at Mexicans comparable to the wrath that was hurled at Asians. That was not because US society found Mexicans to be a uniquely agreeable minority group; it was rather because Mexicans during those years had been relatively unseen. They worked in mining enclaves, sprawling farms and plantations, or remote railroad tracks. Mexican Americans, who comprised minorities in cities and towns of the Southwest, had long been victims of brutal discrimination, but Mexican immigrants were generally spared such treatment. That is, at least, until they became numerous enough to be noticed.

The change took place during the 1920s, when the rate of Mexican immigration greatly increased, and many Mexicans took to entering the country illegally. In fact, prior to 1917 there had never been such a thing as "illegal" immigrant from Mexico, and during World War I Mexicans were exempted from the head tax and literacy test required of other immigrants. The wartime exemptions were such a hit that employers managed to persuade the government to extend them beyond the war's end, but they nonetheless expired in 1922. Adding to Mexicans' woes was the addition of a $10 visa fee to the $8 head tax already charged each entrant, for a total bill of $18 – a princely sum for poor Mexicans. What's more, Mexicans crossing the border legally were made to submit to a humiliating process involving baths and delousing; their heads were shaved, their clothing and baggage taken from them and fumigated, and they were forced to march stark naked before medical inspectors. Small wonder, then, that many Mexicans chose to avoid such irritations and enter the United States surreptitiously. And although their offense was slight – a misdemeanor that, as a favor to southwestern growers, was laxly enforced – it was enough to create an enduring association between Mexican immigrants and criminality in American culture.

Even so, for most of the 1920s, Asians and eastern and southern Europeans continued to bear the brunt of American racism and xenophobia. The movement to restrict immigration had been building steadily since the turn of the century. By 1905 more than a million immigrants were flooding into the United States each year, and some Americans were feeling overwhelmed. In 1907 Congress appointed a commission to study the immigration issue. Chaired by Vermont Republican Senator William P. Dillingham, the commission was made up of dedicated restrictionists. The commission's report, issued in 1911, waxed nostalgic for the northern European immigrants of the early nineteenth century and denounced the more recent crop as decidedly inferior. The commission recommended literacy tests and legal restriction of immigration, especially from southern and eastern Europe. The Dillingham Commission's report, which was the most extensive investigation of immigration carried out to that date, claimed for itself the distinction of being purely scientific in its methods.

World War I tended to reinforce the sense that evil lurked outside of America's boundaries, and more Americans than ever demanded isolation and restriction of immigration. Hostility toward immigrants was, however, selective. The decade or so following World War I witnessed a high tide for the science of eugenics, which held that the human race could be improved by allowing only persons of high moral, physical, and intellectual character to breed – or immigrate – while preventing inferior, unfit persons from doing so. Extreme eugenicists went so far as to oppose most social reform, since, as one writer put it, improving the lives of the downtrodden "tends ultimately to degrade the race by causing an increased survival of the unfit."[1] Eugenics was not based entirely on race – persons with criminal tendencies or with mental retardation, for instance, might be deemed unfit to procreate – but it was inevitably conflated with race and nationality at a time when Americans were increasingly alarmed by the growing heterogeneity of their society. Racial characteristics, in the eugenicists' view, were absolute and biologically determined, so there was no possibility of change or improvement. As one such thinker put it, "Either we must look forward to a new type of race and try on the basis of investigation to predict the qualities and values of that race or we must restrict immigration."[2] Restricting immigration seemed the easier choice.

Eugenicists constructed a hierarchy of races in which non-white peoples were unquestionably inferior, while white Europeans were ranked in their own hierarchy that began with the "Nordic" peoples of northern Europe and descended from there, with the "Mediterranean" whites placing not far above non-white races. Many white, Protestant Americans had come to the conclusion that the United States was founded by and for Nordic peoples, and the presence of other groups among them was dragging down the nation's racial stock. One of the most prominent exponents of these ideas was Madison Grant, whose 1922 book *The Passing of the Great Race* delivered to Americans a grim warning against "race suicide," which in Grant's view was what mingling with the world's degraded peoples would amount to. Grant had no patience with outbursts like the Mexican Revolution, which ostensibly aimed to improve the lot of the poorest Mexicans. "It is called nationalism, patriotism, freedom, and other high-sounding names," Grant sniffed, "but it is everywhere the phenomenon of the long-suppressed, conquered servile classes rising up against the master race." If the Nordic race should permit such riffraff to dwell among them, Grant warned, "then the citadel of civilization will fall for mere lack of defenders."[3] Regulating immigration, then, was no trivial thing. It was a matter of national survival. Such warnings led to the first restrictions on European immigration in an "emergency" immigration restriction act passed in 1921, whereupon Congress began working on a more permanent – and more stringent – measure to restrict immigration.

While racists like Grant did not single out Mexicans for special denunciation, others did not hesitate to do so. By the 1920s the majority of Mexicans were *mestizos*, that is, people of mixed Spanish and Indian ancestry.[4] For racists of the day, this combination was singularly unpromising, for even though it meant that Mexicans were partly white, the white part was of the inferior Mediterranean rather than the Nordic strain, and Indians were clearly classed as racially inferior. The arguments for excluding the entry of such folk into the United States were several. Congressman John C. Box of Texas, who led the anti-Mexican charge in Congress, warned that the American Southwest was committing the very same mistake that the Founding Fathers of the country committed when they sanctioned the institution of slavery. That is, those interests that advocated for unrestricted Mexican immigration were inviting in a wholly unassimilable group that would ensure permanent racial strife. Others were more explicit and colorful in their cataloging of the Mexican's deficiencies. Roy Garis, a professor of economics at

Vanderbilt University, appeared before the House Committee on Immigration to smear Mexicans with a very broad brush indeed, insisting that they had

> minds [that] run to nothing higher than the animal functions – eat, sleep, and sexual debauchery. In every huddle of Mexicans one meets the same idleness, hordes of hungry dogs and filthy children with faces plastered with flies, disease, lice, human filth, stench, promiscuous fornication, bastardy, lounging, apathetic peons and lazy squaws, beans and dried chili, liquor, general squalor, and envy and hatred of the Gringo. These people sleep by day and prowl by night like coyotes, stealing anything they can get their hands on, no matter how useless to them it may be. Nothing left outside is safe unless padlocked or chained down.

Allowing such "human swine" to inhabit the American Southwest, according to Garis, would lower the moral, social, and political character of all Americans, create severe racial problems, and "result in the practical destruction, at least for centuries, of all that is worthwhile in our white civilization."[5]

Not all critics of Mexican immigration were motivated primarily by racial animus. Few groups were more vehement in their calls to restrict immigration than the American Federation of Labor (AFL). The AFL had tried to organize farm labor in California between 1909 and 1914, but abandoned the effort owing largely to the inherent difficulty of organizing an itinerant workforce, resistance from workers to paying the union's high dues, and, probably, race prejudice on the part of the union's leadership. The Industrial Workers of the World (IWW), a far more radical union, also tried to organize the farm workers. But in August 1913 a violent clash between lawmen and IWW-led hop-pickers at Wheatland, California, left four dead and many more wounded, providing the state government a pretext to launch an all-out offensive against the IWW. It was not until the 1930s that communist organizers tried their luck organizing farm workers, and in the meantime – even though the attention brought to the plight of farm workers by the Wheatland Riot led to some efforts to improve their circumstances – those farm workers had few advocates and many enemies.

By the 1920s the AFL had determined that Mexican immigrants constituted a major menace to American workers. The union contended that

Mexicans' willingness to work for low pay pushed down wages for all workers; that Mexicans took jobs that would be done by Americans if a decent wage were offered; and that Mexicans could be used as strike-breakers – a charge that had some force, for Mexicans had in fact been recruited to Chicago to fill in for striking steel workers in 1919 and striking meatpackers in 1921.

Also opposing Mexican immigration on economic grounds were small-scale farmers, as well as farmers from the East and Midwest, who lacked access to cheap Mexican labor and resented the enormous competitive advantage it gave to their rivals in the Southwest.

Nativists and organized labor led the charge against Mexican immigration, and they won support from a bizarre array of interest groups, ranging from the Daughters of the American Revolution, to the American Legion, to the Ku Klux Klan. But these "restrictionists" were sorely overmatched by their opponents, who wielded enormous clout and wanted to ensure that nothing impeded the free flow of Mexican workers to the United States. One of those opponents was the community of United States diplomats, which was slowly warming to the notion that the United States should rethink its policy of bullying Latin Americans, and instead work to cultivate good relations with them. The United States did, after all, have an enormous financial stake in Latin America, and especially in Mexico. Although foreign – and especially United States – domination of the Mexican economy figured among the many causes of the Mexican Revolution of 1910, that domination actually increased in the wake of the revolution, such that by the 1920s foreigners controlled 90 percent of all mining operations in Mexico; most cotton, coffee, and banana plantations; and 94 percent of petroleum operations. Western Hemisphere nations accounted for two thirds of total US foreign investment and one third of US trade, with Mexico the leading player by far. Charles Evans Hughes, who served as US Secretary of State from 1921 to 1925, managed to sway even some staunch Congressional opponents of Mexican immigration by arguing that any restriction on Western Hemisphere immigration would be resented in Latin America, and such resentment could end up harming the US economy.

Wielding far more clout than the diplomats were those powerful interests that benefited from cheap Mexican labor. This group included southwestern growers, railroad and mining concerns, and a handful of industrialists. Their most high profile representatives were the National Grange, the American Farm Bureau Federation, and the United States Chamber of Commerce. These interests were able to marshal some interesting arguments in favor of their position, most of them designed to deflect the charge that they were motivated by narrow self-interest. Mexicans, they contended, did not compete with American workers, because they only took jobs that Americans were unwilling to do. Such jobs, some argued, were not only beneath the dignity of white Americans, but whites were in fact racially unsuited to them. No less an expert that Dr. George P. Clements, manager of the Los Angeles Chamber of Commerce agriculture department from 1917 to 1939, held that farm labor involved the sorts of tasks "to which the oriental and Mexican[,] due to their crouching and bending habits[,] are fully adapted, while the white is physically unable to adapt himself to them."[6] Interestingly, anti-immigration polemicist Madison Grant responded to claims of this sort by asserting that if native-born white Americans were crowded out of menial jobs by swarthy immigrants, they would adapt to the restricted job market by producing fewer offspring. It followed that "the introduction of immigrants as lowly laborers means a replacement of race."[7]

Moreover, it was not merely the employers of that labor who would be hurt if Mexican immigration were to be restricted. Building on their contention that Mexicans were the only workers available for the jobs they performed, a curtailment of their immigration would scuttle the economy of the entire Southwest and harm consumers nationwide, for those consumers would have to pay high prices for their fruits and vegetables, or do without them altogether. Many jobs depended on southwestern agriculture, so a crisis in that sector would cause hardship in many other sectors.

To those who warned of an imminent racial crisis should Mexican immigration be left unrestricted, employer interests responded that Mexicans entered the country temporarily, and would return soon enough to Mexico without doing any serious damage to the racial fabric of the United States. And since, according to those same employers, Mexicans were by nature devoid of ambition, they would not rise in society to the point where they would challenge white dominance. And of course, should Mexicans ever become a problem, the border was close by and they could easily be deported.

Behind all of these practical arguments lay the legal reality that, according to the Treaty of Guadalupe Hidalgo that ended the US–Mexican War, Mexicans living in the formerly Mexican territories that came into the possession of the United States were to automatically receive US citizenship, so long as they did not leave the territory or declare a wish to remain citizens of Mexico. Accordingly, it was not legally feasible to place them in a category with Asians, who were allegedly "unassimilable" people who were legally ineligible for US citizenship and hence legitimate targets of discrimination. The point had been decisively established in 1896 when an impoverished Mexican named Ricardo Rodríguez, who had lived in San Antonio, Texas, for ten years, applied to the federal district court for US citizenship. The resulting case, which came after a prolonged effort on the part of many white Texans to disenfranchise all Mexicans and people of Mexican descent in Texas, attracted considerable popular interest. The court ruled that Rodríguez – and, by extension, all Mexicans – was entitled to US citizenship.

The restrictionist impulse led ultimately to the passage of the Immigration Act of 1924, also known as the Johnson-Reed Act, which followed many of the recommendations made in the 1911 Dillingham Commission report. At the time of the debates over the 1924 Act, Mexicans were considered legally "white." That fact, together with the labor needs of southwestern growers and US diplomatic concerns, effectively trumped the arguments of nativists and organized labor: no quotas were established for Mexico, nor for the rest of the nations of the Western Hemisphere.

This is not to say that the Immigration Act of 1924 is irrelevant to the story of Mexican immigration to the United States. The Act began with the premise that the dominant racial strain in the United States was, and should remain, "Nordic." Since Asians were already barred from immigrating by the Immigration Act of 1917 – a point that the 1924 Act upheld – the 1924 Act was aimed principally at restricting immigration of southern and eastern Europeans. The law established a "national origins quota system" that limited immigration of persons of any given nationality to 2 percent of the number of persons of that nationality who had resided in the United States in 1890, as revealed by the census of that year. As intended, this Act severely curtailed the immigration of Europeans, adding to the shortages of unskilled labor that southwestern employers had been moaning about for years, further cementing the position of Mexicans as the dominant source of agricultural labor in the Southwest. Southwestern employers swore they had no choice but to entice Mexicans across the border. As one wealthy rancher complained in 1928, "We have no Chinamen, we have no Japs. The Hindu is worthless, the Filipino is nothing, and the white man will not do the work."[8]

The 1924 Act also created a Border Patrol, although in this early incarnation the agency hardly presented a formidable obstacle to border crossers. By 1930 it had only 723 agents to patrol the borders with both Canada and Mexico, and these agents were frequently of low quality – many were affiliated with the Ku Klux Klan, and training was non-existent. During the 1920s the Border Patrol was chiefly concerned with enforcing customs laws and obstructing the smuggling of bootleg liquor.

Depression and Deportation in the 1930s

By the late 1920s the increased numbers and heightened profile of Mexican immigrants – coupled with an ongoing tide of nativism among Americans – led to increased calls to restrict Mexican immigration. Organized labor remained a leading voice calling for restriction, especially since the AFL planned a major organizing drive in the Southwest in early 1925, which would likely be imperiled by continued high levels of migration from Mexico. The AFL experimented with diplomacy as a means to curtail immigration, working with its Mexican counterpart, the Regional Confederation of Mexican Workers (CROM). AFL leaders tried to persuade CROM leaders to press the Mexican government to take strenuous measures to discourage the emigration of Mexican citizens to the United States. A conference was held to discuss these matters in Washington, DC in August 1925, but the delegates to the conference talked past one another. The American delegates wanted to discuss curbing immigration, but the Mexican delegates were far more concerned with getting assurances that Mexican citizens would be treated well and fairly while in the United States. In subsequent years the AFL did manage to persuade the CROM to advocate for legislation restricting Mexican emigration, but by then the CROM's power had waned. In all, the AFL's efforts bore little fruit, so other measures had to be tried if Mexican immigration were to be restricted.

Although no numerical restrictions were imposed on Western Hemisphere immigration during the 1920s, new administrative restrictions were imposed on Mexican immigration in the late 1920s that made immigration more difficult. In March 1929 Congress passed legislation that made illegal entry a misdemeanor punishable by a $1,000 fine or up to a year in prison, or both; a second such offense was made a felony, punishable with up to two years' imprisonment and a fine of $2,000. At the same time, the State Department told US consuls in Mexico to become more stringent in their criteria for granting immigration visas, denying visas to illiterates, persons deemed likely to become "public charges," and persons who held labor contracts, which violated an 1885 law forbidding the contracting of labor in foreign lands with specific promises of employment. Also in the late 1920s, the Border Patrol was enlarged and ordered to "crack down" on unauthorized immigration from Mexico. These policies succeeded in bringing about a sharp decline in the volume of immigration at the southern border.

The news was not all bleak for undocumented immigrants, however. In 1929 Congress passed the so-called Registry Act, which allowed unauthorized immigrants who could prove they had lived in the United States continuously since before June 3, 1921, and that they were of good character, to legalize their status. Chambers of Commerce and other business groups energetically informed Mexican workers of their new rights and helped them with their applications, but even so, the largest number of applications came from European immigrants, who accounted for some 80 percent of those whose status was regularized.

The increasingly stringent policies of the late 1920s had some effect, but a far more serious curtailment of migration was brought about by the US stock market crash of October 1929 and the brutal economic shock of the Great Depression. Mexicans in the United States suffered disproportionately, for not only were foreigners the first workers dismissed in hard times, but they were widely scapegoated for those hard times. Chambers of commerce, which during the 1920s had been among the most outspoken champions of unrestricted immigration, now urged factories to fire their foreign workers first. In short order, perhaps half of all Mexican workers in the United States found themselves unemployed and in desperate straits. The oversupply of labor was especially serious in agriculture, still the primary employer of Mexican laborers. Many cities and states passed ordinances barring foreigners from working on public works projects, ousting Mexicans from construction jobs that some had held for more than a decade. In California vigilantes threatened violence against any businesses that hired Mexicans in preference to Americans.

The anti-Mexican sentiment that had been building throughout the 1920s now reached a crescendo. The Arizona legislature, in a 1930 resolution demanding quotas on Mexican immigration, charged that Mexicans were "making beggars and tramps of many of our native-born citizens because of an oversupply of labor," and further that many Mexicans were "afflicted with infectious and loathsome diseases, and thousands ... are saturated with Bolshevik doctrines, thus becom[ing] an actual menace and danger to our institutions and Government."[9]

Among those who charged that immigrants were largely responsible for the unemployment problem was no less a figure than President Herbert Hoover. During the 1920s Hoover, as Secretary of Commerce, had lent his voice to the movement opposing quotas on Mexican immigration. Hoover was closely allied with prominent business interests who depended heavily on cheap Mexican labor; he also chaired the Inter-American High Commission, a trade organization, and fretted that restricting Mexican immigration might adversely affect US trade with Latin America. But the advent of the Depression caused Hoover, together with most business people, to have a change of heart. In 1930 Hoover appointed William Doak as Labor Secretary. Doak soon distinguished himself for his anti-immigrant zeal, wildly exaggerating the numbers of illegal immigrants in the country and suggesting that the solution to the unemployment problem lay in booting foreigners out. Doak unleashed agents to carry out raids on private homes and public places across the United States in hopes of frightening immigrants into departing voluntarily.

The anti-immigrant campaign was especially intense in southern California, which had the nation's highest concentration of Mexican immigrants, and where city leaders were thinking along the same likes as Secretary Doak. In particular, Charles Visel, director of the Los Angeles Committee on Coordination of Unemployment Relief, shared Doak's conviction that ousting immigrants was the key to solving the unemployment problem. Visel was outdone by Los Angeles police chief Roy Steckel, who claimed that ousting immigrants would also solve the city's crime problem. Visel heartily embraced the idea of using scare tactics to send immigrants packing and to free up jobs (he even invented a word – "scareheading" – to describe this practice). The strategy was to have several men from the US Department of Labor come to Los Angeles and preside over a few arrests, ensuring that those arrests received ample publicity, and thus creating a climate so hostile that immigrants would gladly depart. William F. Watkins, a supervisor for the Bureau of Immigration, arrived in Los Angeles along with 18 immigration agents at the end of January 1931, and quickly embraced Visel's scheme. Soon, immigration agents and local police were carrying out a string of well-publicized raids, and detaining and questioning thousands of persons they suspected of being in the country illegally. In the end, 230 people were deported and another 159 agreed to leave voluntarily. Seventy percent of the deportees were Mexicans.

The scare campaign seems to have had a negligible effect on freeing up jobs for US citizens. Apparently few of those involved in the effort fully appreciated the contradiction at the heart of their strategy, for a large number of those immigrants who fled were already unemployed, so their departure could have had but little impact on the rate of joblessness. But the campaign was wildly successful at causing Mexicans to flee. While the immigration agents requested fewer than 400 warrants, an estimated 40,000 Mexicans left the country of their own accord. Soon the dusty border towns of Mexicali and Tijuana were so choked with repatriated Mexicans that the Mexican government sent a formal request that the returnees be routed to other cities. Tijuana, at the time, was a rude village with a population under 20,000. Prior to the 1950s it was unconnected to the rest of Mexico by roads or railroads, its primary purpose being to cater to the whims of Americans seeking the illicit amusements of sex, drugs, liquor, and gambling. The town was wholly unprepared for the sudden influx of returning migrants, and serious social problems quickly arose. The United States replied that the people flooding into the border towns were not actually deportees, but it also took the point, and subsequently efforts were made to channel returning migrants toward other border cities such as El Paso and Nogales.

Alongside the scare campaign of 1931 was another, unrelated effort carried out in cities across the United States to repatriate Mexicans. These campaigns were undertaken by city and county welfare bureaus and private charities that were principally concerned with the burden of unemployed Mexicans on relief. Los Angeles welfare officials estimated that unemployed Mexicans were costing the city at least $200,000 per month; compared to that, the cost of deporting them was a relative bargain. Mexicans with little hope of finding employment were amenable enough to the offer of repatriation, for if nothing else it would give them an all-expense paid trip to visit family in Mexico. Repatriates were offered free transportation to El Paso or Nogales, plus food, clothing, and medical care. The Mexican government did its part by offering free rail transport from the border to the interior, charging repatriates no duties on cars, trucks, tools, appliances, and whatever else they might bring with them from the United States. Among the repatriates were a considerable number of US citizens, particularly the children of immigrants who had been born and raised in the United States and who had much difficulty adjusting to life in Mexico. By the mid-1930s the pace of repatriation had declined considerably, mostly owing to Franklin Roosevelt's policies of providing federal funds to local welfare programs and sponsoring massive public works projects, both of which eased the burden on local relief agencies. There is no reliable figure on the total number of Mexicans repatriated during the 1930s, though most estimates hover around 150,000.

The Fate of the Repatriates

Repatriated Mexicans returned to Mexico to find ongoing hardship in their home country, and they in turn added to the already existing surplus of labor. The natural increase in Mexico's population was more than 50 percent during the 1930s, and repatriates swelled that population increase by another 10 percent. In the north-central region of the country – the source of the majority of immigrants to the United States – corn prices doubled as agricultural production fell to pre-revolutionary levels and Mexico was forced to import large quantities of corn and wheat. Returning migrants also faced the fact that no one could agree quite what to make of them. Repatriates came home to a certain amount of suspicion that, having tasted the good life, they might now find Mexico sadly wanting, and might therefore threaten the nation's political stability. Some saw Mexicans who had left as traitors who had abandoned their homeland, and who now came back – some of them, anyway – flaunting their newfound worldliness. This was a popular theme in Mexican *corridos* (folk songs) of the era. For example, in a corrido called "The Renegade," the singer excoriates repatriates thus: "… they learn a little American / And dress up like dudes / And go to the dance / But he who denies his race / Is the most miserable creature / There is nothing in the world so vile as he / The mean figure of the renegade."[10]

Others enthusiastically encouraged emigrants to return to Mexico as a patriotic gesture, employing the money, goods, and new skills they had presumably acquired in the United States for the betterment of Mexico rather than to help out its overbearing neighbor. The famous muralist Diego Rivera was in this category. During the early 1930s he was in Detroit working on the "Detroit Industry Murals" at the Detroit Institute of Arts. He collaborated with the Mexican consul to form a "League of Mexican Workers and Peasants," which arranged for the repatriation of Mexican factory workers and worked to protect their civil rights in the process. Rivera assured returning migrants that the Mexican government, in its benevolence, would do all it could to smooth their homecoming.

In fact, there were some attempts to ease the transition of the returning migrants and to help them find a productive place in Mexican society, though none of these efforts was notably successful. In late 1932 a group of government officials, business people, and charitable organizations founded the National Repatriation Committee. This group reasoned that the repatriates would be best served by founding new agricultural communities, where land could be purchased on easy terms over long periods. The colonies were to be located far from the US border, on the theory that migrants near the border might be tempted to work for a spell in Mexico and then slip back into the United States to partake of the higher wages to be had there.

The group collected donations and founded two colonies, one a very small affair near Acapulco, the other a more ambitious undertaking known as Pinotepa Nacional, which was located on the coast of the southern state of Oaxaca. This newly created colony was populated at first by some 400 repatriates, and their numbers swelled to around 700 by the spring of 1933. Unfortunately, the colony had its share of problems. Its location was notoriously unhealthy. In a single 20-day period, 60 people died from disease, and survivors were bedeviled by black flies and sand fleas that caused severe itching, inflammation, and possible infection. By most accounts, the leaders of the colony were nearly as obnoxious as the vermin, for colonists complained that administrators allowed the colonists no say in governance, rationed food cruelly, and punished any who protested. Most supplies had to come by ship, and the ships were notoriously unreliable. The colonists voted with their feet, such that by February 1934 only 8 colonists remained (tellingly, those 8 were governed by 15 administrators). The National Repatriation Committee was dissolved in June 1934, after an existence of only 15 months.

The National Repatriation Committee was replaced by a National Repatriation Board, a governmental organization with representatives from the ministries of agriculture, foreign relations, economy, interior, public health, and labor, as well as the National Bank of Agricultural Credit. This was scarcely more successful than its predecessor, for by the time the National Repatriation Board swung into action, the flow of repatriates was tapering dramatically. The board planned a few "model colonies," but that is about as far as things went.

During the 1930s the Mexican government began to develop massive irrigation projects just across the US border, aiming to create vast plantations that would grow cotton, wheat, sorghum, and other crops, largely for the US market. The project was partly inspired by the thinking of anthropologist Manuel Gamio, who noted that central and southern Mexico tended to be more indigenous, and hence those southerners were, in Gamio's view, more encumbered by stultifying traditions and prejudices. Moreover, those southerners had been beaten down by centuries of oppression, discrimination, and malnutrition, and could only be redeemed by a drastic transformation of their diets, outlooks, and environment. The people of the north, Gamio argued, tended to be whiter, taller, healthier, and more progressive in their outlook. Gamio assumed that Mexicans who had lived and worked in the United States had learned valuable skills and imbibed progressive views and healthy work discipline while in that country, which could be valuable assets to Mexico's development if the government could harness those gains productively. If returning migrants had historically made scant contributions to Mexican development, Gamio reasoned, it was mostly because they had returned to their home communities and been quickly seduced back to the habitual torpor of those communities. Ironically, then, while the National Repatriation Committee had recommended that repatriates be isolated from the northern border, Gamio advised that they be located in border enclaves so they would be isolated from their fellow Mexicans.

In 1926 the Mexican National Irrigation Commission was organized, its goal to transform wasteland into valuable cropland, just as had been done nearly three decades earlier in the southwestern United States. Manuel Gamio was, at that very moment, in the United States carrying out a study of Mexican migration funded by the Social Science Research Council, and he made a priority of exploring how irrigation projects could create new opportunities for repatriates. Gamio interviewed many immigrants in hopes of finding just the right elements for new agricultural colonies to be founded on public lands near the border.

The government did indeed construct massive hydraulic works in northern Mexico. The most impressive of these was the Río Salado Irrigation System, also known as the Don Martín Dam, in the easternmost part of the state of Coahuila. Completed in 1930, the dam brought nearly 150,000 acres of formerly arid land in Coahuila and Nuevo León into cultivation by 1935.

Lázaro Cárdenas, a left-leaning populist, campaigned for the presidency in 1934 on a platform of radical land reform, pro-labor policies, and Mexican nationalism. Cárdenas saw attracting Mexicans back to Mexico as closely related to his other initiatives, for he fully shared Dr. Gamio's conviction that Mexican emigrants were likely to have acquired special skills during their sojourn in the United States – for instance, the proper use of fertilizers and pesticides, the workings of modern farm machinery, and management of soil and irrigation works, as well as sound financial habits – and if Mexico could entice such enlightened individuals into returning home they would be invaluable assets to Mexico's own agricultural development.

Upon winning the presidency, Cárdenas made aid to repatriates part of the Six-Year Plan of the National Revolutionary Party, the official party in what had effectively become a single party state. By 1936 Cárdenas was delivering regular radio speeches inviting Mexicans to return to their "mother country," and in response he received many letters from desperate people asking for assistance.

Cárdenas's preoccupation with other issues seems to have precluded his acting on these initiatives until the summer of 1939, when he sent his Under-Secretary of Foreign Affairs, Ramón Beteta, on a mission to visit Mexicans throughout the United States and make bold promises of immediate and very generous aid to any migrants who were willing to return home. Specifically, Beteta promised that the Mexican government would foot the bill for transportation from the United States to the repatriates' final destination; allow duty-free entry of all cars, animals, machinery, and other goods acquired in the United States; provide 20 acres of irrigated land or 50 acres of unirrigated land in colonies in Sinaloa, Tamaulipas, or Baja California; and furnish financial support for one year, after which bank loans and private credit would become available.

Beteta should have had considerable credibility: the scion of a wealthy landowning family, he boasted a degree in economics from the University of Texas, and both a law degree and a doctorate in social science from the National Autonomous University of Mexico. He was also very close to President Cárdenas. Beteta launched his trip at a tense time, for Cárdenas had angered some powerful people the year before when he suddenly decreed the confiscation of the assets of all foreign oil companies operating in Mexico. Officials of the Franklin D. Roosevelt administration saw Beteta's goodwill tour as a way to ease tensions while wholeheartedly endorsing his goal of luring Mexicans back home. Beteta was feted enthusiastically as he visited many US cities, but contrary to all expectations he found few takers for his proffered largess.

In response to that recalcitrance, Beteta's promises became increasingly generous. He said people could delay accepting aid for six months to a year, allowing them to get their affairs in order before relocating; at one point he even extended the offer of aid and land to non-Mexicans. He trumpeted the founding of a new colony near the border to be called Colonia 18 de Marzo, in honor of the date upon which the oil expropriation was decreed, assuring that 800,000 pesos were being set aside for the project.

For all this effort, only about 5,000 people took the offer, and most of those who did were the poorest of the poor, the very antithesis of the progressive, well-trained agriculturists men like Manuel Gamio had envisioned. The project seems to have been undone by a generalized mistrust of government promises, fears of the enormous adjustments that would have to be made in adopting a new way of life in a newly created colony, and an uneasy sense that, as bad as things were in the United States, they were likely worse in Mexico.

Labor Unrest

American employers had long held that the most appealing traits that Mexicans possessed were their loyalty and their docility. Events of the early 1930s suggest that those employers were engaging in a bit of wishful thinking.

At a time when many Americans were suffering unprecedented hardship, immigrant workers were often targeted for special immiseration. In California's Imperial Valley, one of the most productive agricultural regions in the world, shipments of cantaloupes and lettuce declined by more than 50 percent between 1929 and 1933, while wages paid to farm workers fell from 35 cents an hour to 14 cents an hour. A 1935 study in California found that the average migrant farm worker family earned about $289 per year, at a time when it was estimated that mere subsistence for a family of four required $780 per year, and average family income was $1,784 per year. By the mid-1930s, impoverished refugees from the Dust Bowl of the Great Plains – white people who were willing to take any job, no matter how menial – were flooding into California. By 1933, even after the repatriation of some 1.5 million Mexican workers, there were still two workers for every available farm job in California. In San Antonio, Texas, wages paid to Mexican pecan shellers were so low – about $192 per year – that even though the process could readily have been mechanized, pecan growers reasoned that tedious hand-shelling brought greater profits.

Farm workers – including a high proportion of Mexican immigrants – had been showing signs of militancy since 1928, when delegates met in Los Angeles to form the Confederation of Mexican Labor Unions, a union modeled on Mexico's CROM. The union's most active local could be found in California's Imperial Valley, where cantaloupe workers demanded a better wage, drinking water, lumber to build sheds, accident indemnity, and withholding of wages by the growers instead of by labor contractors. When growers disregarded these demands, the union went on strike. Growers and their allies – and they had many allies in politics and law enforcement – waged a no-holds-barred effort to crush the strike, arresting dozens on charges of vagrancy and disturbing the peace, raiding and shutting down union offices, and threatening mass deportation. The strike was broken within days.

The dismal fate of the 1928 cantaloupe workers' strike did not dissuade other workers from following suit. In California the early 1930s witnessed more than 140 agricultural strikes, most demanding higher pay. Active in organizing these strikes was the Trade Union Unity League (TUUL), a "revolutionary industrial union" affiliated with the American Communist Party. The communists – like the anarchist Industrial Workers of the World before them – slipped into the void left by the mainstream American Federation of Labor, which had long since written off farm workers as both unorganizable and not worth organizing. The Communist Party, by contrast, actively courted Mexican workers with promises of higher wages, better treatment, and complete racial equality. The labor movement also reached out to Filipino, East Indian, Japanese, and Chinese farm workers, hoping to promote class solidarity over ethnic antagonism. This would be no mean feat, given that growers had for decades used ethnicity as a wedge to divide and weaken workers by playing off one ethnic group against another. The TUUL organized a union specifically devoted to farm worker issues, giving it the unwieldy title of Cannery and Agricultural Workers' Industrial Union, or C&AWIU.

One major problem for the C&AWIU, and any other group that aspired to organize farm workers, was that the growers were very well organized indeed, and had been for some time. Growers had long since come to appreciate the advantages of acting in concert with one another. In 1917 the Valley Fruit Growers Association of Fresno brought some 3,000 growers together to organize the distribution of farm labor. In 1926 an agricultural labor bureau was organized in San Joaquin City to help farmers control labor, while in southern California an agricultural producers' labor committee performed a similar function for growers of walnuts, avocados, citrus fruits, and vegetables.

One of the key problems that these associations addressed was how to keep wages uniform and low despite the dramatic fluctuations in labor demand that characterize agriculture. During harvest time, when demand for labor peaked, workers might take advantage of the sudden spike in their bargaining power. Lack of grower solidarity could be very costly, as some farmers might, in their desperation to get the crop picked, pirate workers from other farmers with offers of higher wages. The solution to this, of course, was for growers to meet before the harvest season and decide what wage they would be paying. In 1934 the various grower organizations of California coalesced into the Associated Farmers, which, in addition to labor management and wage fixing, aimed, in the words of its constitution, "to foster and encourage respect for and to maintain law and order, to promote the prompt, orderly and efficient administration of justice." This was a euphemistic way of saying that the Associated Farmers was dedicated to organizing anti-labor propaganda and violence. As one observer put it in 1947, "California's industrial agriculture can exhibit all the customary weapons ... gas, goon squads, propaganda, bribery."[11]

Undaunted, the C&AWIU appeared in California in 1930, and it began its activity in November 1932 by organizing a strike among fruit pickers near Vacaville, California. The fruit pickers' strike held out for two months against beatings and threats administered by some 180 armed, deputized vigilantes. Pea pickers and cherry pickers struck in April 1933 to protest their starvation wage of 12 cents per hour, and despite a campaign of arrests, beatings, and intimidation, they succeeded in winning a small wage increase.

The first major action involving the C&AWIU took place in June 1933 at El Monte, in the San Gabriel Valley of California. Somewhat ironically, the strike involved ethnicity in unaccustomed ways, pitting Mexican berry pickers against mainly Japanese growers who had managed, through various forms of subterfuge, to acquire large amounts of land despite the 1913 Alien Land Law barring them from land ownership. The strike was initiated by the Confederation of Mexican Labor Unions, which demanded that wages be increased to 25 cents per hour (they had been 9–10 cents per hour). Soon the C&AWIU entered the scene, and the strike incorporated onion and celery workers from nearby fields, eventually involving some 7,000 workers. When the Japanese growers offered to raise wages to 20 cents per hour, recognize the Mexican union, and dismiss strikebreakers, the workers acquiesced and returned to the fields, despite protests from C&AWIU leaders.

In October 1933 the C&AWIU began agitating among cotton pickers in the San Joaquin Valley of California, who had seen their pay drop by more than 60 percent between the late 1920s and early 1930s. When once again growers ignored the union's demand for a pay hike, the workers struck. This time the strike involved about 12,000 workers, 70 percent of them Mexican, and covered over 100,000 acres, making it, by most accounts, the largest agricultural strike in US history. Once again, the growers responded ruthlessly, evicting workers from their makeshift hovels on grower land, arresting picketers, and waging a campaign of terror and intimidation. On October 10, three men were murdered and nine more were injured by gunshot wounds. Two days later, as union members were meeting in Pixley, California, a large number of cars pulled up outside the meeting hall and opened fire indiscriminately on the strikers, killing two men and wounding several more. The vigilantes continued firing even as the unarmed strikers retreated in panic. State Highway Patrol cars pulled up as the firing diminished, doing nothing for several minutes as the shooters drove off. Eventually, the police roused themselves to stop the vigilante party and confiscate their weapons, but they made no arrests. Another worker was murdered in a separate incident the same day. Later, nine growers were arrested in the incident; sympathetic locals promptly acquitted them of all charges.

The adversity seemed only to embolden the strikers. Evicted from their homes, strikers formed tent camps, including one at Corcoran, which contained 4,300 people with no water or sanitary facilities and where nine infants died of malnutrition during the strike. As mass starvation threatened, the state government stepped in to provide emergency relief, making it clear that such relief would be available only if the strikers compromised on their wage demands. Adding his voice to these demands was the Mexican consul, Enrique Bravo, who urged the strikers to take whatever was offered and warned of "grave international complications" should they fail to do so. By the end of October, strikers began

Figure 2.1 In the early 1930s, Mexican farm workers engaged in a series of strikes aimed at improving their wages and working conditions. Here farm workers gather at the strike headquarters during the 1933 cotton strike at Corcoran, California, to demand the right to organize and bargain collectively. Courtesy of the Bancroft Library, University of California, Berkeley.

to return to the fields, and the strike – which had lasted a little over three weeks – came to an inglorious end.

As yet undaunted, the C&AWIU called another strike in the Imperial Valley in early 1934, this one centered on lettuce workers. An early mass meeting at El Centro was dispersed with tear gas bombs and beatings. The strike was definitively crushed on February 19, when vigilantes raided a workers' encampment with fire and tear gas, forcing 2,000 men, women, and children to flee for their lives and leaving one baby dead from the fumes. A National Labor Relations Board investigation disclosed wholesale violations of civil rights and the appalling misery of the workers, including "filth, squalor, an entire absence of sanitation, and a crowding of human beings into totally inadequate tents or crude structures built of boards, weeds, and anything that was at hand to give a pitiful semblance of a home at its worst. Words cannot describe some of the conditions we saw."[12] One federal labor conciliator had his phone tapped, his mail opened, and his life threatened.

The movement died with a whimper in July 1934, when the union tried to call a general strike at San Francisco, only to have the strike broken by the National Guard and what journalist and activist Carey McWilliams called "a statewide reign of terror" involving hundreds of arrests and beatings. The headquarters of the C&AWIU was raided by men with sawed-off shotguns, rubber hoses, handcuffs, blackjacks, and tear gas bombs. Eighteen of the union's top leaders were arrested and charged with "criminal syndicalism," a catch-all category that could be, and was, loosely interpreted by the authorities and the courts. Eight of the C&AWIU leaders were convicted and jailed, and although they were released after two years, the union was defunct.

Outside of California, migrant labor organizing was scarce but not unknown. In the early 1930s the most miserable wages in the United States were paid to the 10,000 to 20,000 Mexican pecan shellers working in the vicinity of San Antonio, Texas. The going rate for pecan shelling was 5–6 cents for every pound of pecans shelled. The average worker was able to shell eight or nine pounds of pecans per day, for a sum total of not more than 54 cents for a full day's work. The average pecan shelling family had to make do with about $192 per year, a wage so insignificant that, even though the pecan shelling business could easily have been mechanized, growers determined that the matter was more profitably left to the Mexicans. And profits were handsome indeed. The largest of the Texas pecan men, Julius Seligman, was making more than $3 million a year by the mid-1930s. The growers' greed was, if anything, exceeded by their arrogance, which inspired them to disregard the dictate of the National Recovery Administration that a $6 per day minimum wage should be paid to pecan shellers.

Late in 1937 the Mexican pecan shellers of San Antonio began to organize under the auspices of the newly founded United Cannery, Agricultural, Packing and Allied Workers of America, a union affiliated with the Congress of Industrial Organizations. In early 1938, when their wage was cut even further, 12,000 pecan shellers spontaneously walked off the job. Local authorities arrested about 1,000 picketers on charges of unlawful assembly and disturbing the peace, and tear gas was liberally employed to disrupt picket lines. The governor of Texas set up an arbitration board that set the wage at 55–65 cents per pound, but hot on the heels of that ruling the Fair Labor Standards Act was passed mandating a minimum wage of 25 cents per hour. Rather than pay that sum, the growers closed up shop, installed machinery, and reopened with a tiny fraction of the workforce they had previously employed.

The labor actions of the 1930s brought little in the way of material improvement for Mexican workers. They may, however, have brought some attention to the plight of agricultural workers in burgeoning agribusiness operations, and at least in a small way they may have helped to belie the curiously enduring myth that Mexicans were docile creatures, happy to endure any abuse. And one observer of those events would go on to accomplish great things. It was during the 1930s that a young César Chávez – the son of a moderately successful immigrant family devastated by the Great Depression – began working in the California bean fields with his family. In 1962 César Chávez organized the United Farm Workers, the first successful farm workers' union in American history.

3

The Bracero Era
1942–1964

The 1940s mark a sharp turning point in the history of both Mexico and the United States, and the dramatic changes of those years ushered in a new era in the history of Mexican immigration to the United States. The United States' entry into World War II ended the Great Depression and created a labor shortage in agriculture, as some 10 million men were conscripted into the military and war industries boomed, leaving once again a dire shortage of labor for US agriculture. Mexicans, who had been reviled and expelled during the lean years, were suddenly in high demand – so much so that big farmers realized that they did not have the capacity to recruit the numbers they needed. Nor could they advocate simply opening the border and allowing Mexicans to gravitate toward whatever work they found most agreeable and remunerative, for those workers would most likely eschew agriculture. What they needed was a rapid, tightly controlled migration. Realizing that only one entity had the wherewithal to perform such a feat, the growers, who had always spurned government interference in their affairs, were obliged reluctantly to rethink that position. Thus was born, in 1942, the "Bracero Program," a long-lived experiment in planned and managed migration that would eventually bring some 4.5 million Mexicans legally to the United States, even while helping to greatly increase the flow of undocumented workers.

Beyond Borders: A History of Mexican Migration to the United States
By Timothy J. Henderson
© 2011 Timothy J. Henderson

Many Mexicans were eager to participate in the Bracero Program, since for the vast majority of people conditions in Mexico did not improve, and in many ways they deteriorated, after the official end of the Depression. Much of the misery Mexicans experienced was created by the unwise choices made by the politicians of Mexico's single party state, aided and abetted by foreign foundations and corporations.

Unbalanced Development in the 1940s

During the 1920s the regimes that had triumphed in the Mexican Revolution began haltingly to try to fulfill the "promises of the revolution." Chief among those promises, given the high levels of peasant participation in the conflict, was land reform. Peasants demanded land, and many resorted to violent means to get it. The process was brutal and slow, but many thousands of peasants eventually received land in the form of *ejidos*, or communally owned and administered farmlands.

During the late 1930s, President Lázaro Cárdenas carried out the most sweeping agrarian reform yet seen in Latin America. His administration expropriated more than 44 million acres of land from large estates – nearly half of all cultivable land in Mexico – and distributed them among 811,000 peasants. Most of these *ejidos* were village-based farmlands, but in areas that were known for large-scale commercial farming – such as the extensive and modern cotton plantation complex in the La Laguna region in the states of Durango and Coahuila – cooperative farms known as "collective *ejidos*" were created to take advantage of economies of scale. In 1936 Cárdenas established a National Ejido Credit Bank to provide the *ejidos* with credit and technical assistance; by 1940 the bank had invested 300 million pesos toward *ejido* development. In that same year, the *ejidos* accounted for 52 percent of the value of Mexico's agricultural output. Many problems remained in Mexican agriculture, most especially the fact that nearly nine out of ten farmers still eked out a bare subsistence on small plots of rocky, rain fed land. Still, had Cárdenas's course been pursued by succeeding governments, Mexico might well have developed a prosperous and productive rural middle class.

Unfortunately, the leaders who came after Cárdenas had starkly different priorities. Mexico's official party – known as the Institutional

Revolutionary Party (PRI) from 1946 onward – was a closed corporation, where advancement normally occurred not through political competition, but through graft and cronyism. The men who ascended to the party's top ranks – all of them civilians after 1946 – were middle- and upper-class city dwellers who were beguiled by the notion of modernity. They dreamed of transforming Mexico into an advanced, powerful, urban, industrial nation. Agriculture, in their view, existed to subsidize the needs of industry and city folk. It must, therefore, be highly commercial and highly productive. Post-1940 party leaders disdained the *ejidos*, which they viewed as primitive and unpromising. They channeled the lion's share of public financing toward large farms, most of them in the north of the country and belonging mostly to families of high-ranking politicians and well-connected businessmen.

The framers of Mexico's revolutionary Constitution of 1917, mindful of how over-concentration of land in few hands had served as a spark for the revolution, had capped the size of a single private land holding at 247 acres of irrigated land or 494 acres of unirrigated land, but those limits presented little obstacle. Landowners simply made a fictitious division of their holdings among various kinfolk and friends, while operating the holdings as single farms. In the Yaquí Valley of Sonora in northwestern Mexico, for instance, nearly 117,000 acres of the richest irrigated land belonged to only 85 individuals, though it was registered under 1,191 different names. Funding for development of rural infrastructure, credit, and mechanization was showered on those fortunate few.

Tedious though they may be, a few statistics can help to put the matter into relief. Between 1941 and 1952, fully 90 percent of Mexico's agricultural budget went to large irrigation projects in a handful of northern states, and nearly all of the suddenly valuable land that resulted from those projects quickly found its way into the hands of wealthy, well-connected entrepreneurs. Large farmers owned a mere 3 percent of all agricultural properties, yet they owned 84 percent of all land in the private (non-*ejidal*) sector. Large and medium sized farmers represented only 7 percent of those who derived income from farming in Mexico, yet they took in 46 percent of net agricultural income. By 1960 a mere 1.3 percent of all farms in Mexico accounted for 54 percent of the volume of production. The Agricultural Credit Bank, originally envisioned as a source of low-interest loans to small farmers, had its available funds increased nearly 13-fold in the late 1940s, and restrictions against lending to large landowners were abolished. The bank was transformed into a cash cow for the already well to do. With free-flowing credit, large farmers were able to mechanize their operations, and to participate in a well-intentioned, albeit ultimately catastrophic, experiment in increasing agricultural productivity known as the "Green Revolution."

The Green Revolution was sponsored by the Rockefeller Foundation, which began its experiments in 1943. American and Mexican scientists worked together to develop new, more productive seed strains, fertilizers, and chemicals to eradicate insects and plant diseases. The Mexican government and private investors poured billions into research and infrastructure improvements. The results were, in some ways, quite spectacular, a dramatic increase in farm output that became part of what admiring observers soon dubbed the "Mexican Miracle." Between 1940 and 1960, Mexico's agricultural output increased at an average rate of 6.3 percent per year, one of the highest rates of increase in the world.

The problem with the Green Revolution was that it reinforced all of the skewed development priorities of the Mexican regime. Green Revolution technologies – mostly fossil fuel based fertilizers and pesticides – were of no use to the vast majority of Mexico's farmers, for only those with access to ample quantities of capital, land, and water were able to take advantage of them. The Green Revolution brought about a rise in overall productivity, but it badly exacerbated the existing class and regional divide that was already the bane of modern Mexico. By 1970 nearly half of all public funds for irrigation projects were used to bring some 2.5 million acres of irrigated land into cultivation in only four northern states, which were home to only just above 9 percent of Mexico's population. Meanwhile, six states in the north-central region of the country – not coincidentally, the states that sent the largest numbers of migrants to the United States – which contained more than a quarter of Mexico's total population, got only 15 percent of irrigation investment, and brought only a half million acres of irrigated land into cultivation.

Meanwhile, the supposed beneficiaries of Mexico's revolutionary agrarian reform – the so-called *ejidatarios*, with their communally owned lands – found themselves pushed to the sidelines as their more prosperous countrymen grew flush. The dominant ideology of the Mexican government after 1940 celebrated capitalism and individualism, and its leaders decided that the collective and communal experiments of the 1930s were folly. Even though evidence has shown that, all things being equal, *ejidos* were actually more productive than the large farms, all things were not equal. Mexico's government leaders, blinded by ideology, prophesied that the *ejidos* would be unproductive, and then set about systematically making sure that prophecy would be fulfilled. The *ejidos* received scandalously few resources. Even the collective *ejidos*, which emerged as large and highly productive commercial farms during the late 1930s, were deliberately sabotaged by the government, as it privileged private farmers at every turn and thus ensured that the collectives would fail. The less commercial *ejidos* fared far worse. They formed the base of a nightmarishly complex and unresponsive bureaucracy that sought primarily to use the *ejidatarios* – who, after all, owed their ownership of land to the "revolution" – as subordinated, tightly controlled pawns of an increasingly centralized and authoritarian state.

Also benefiting little from government policies were the 900,000 or so private farmers who scratched out a bare living growing scrawny stalks of corn on 12 acres or less of dry, rocky land, who had little access to credit or technology or education, who faced a monopoly market for farm goods, and who had nothing to do for most of the year. These were not counted among the unemployed, as it was assumed they had at least the wherewithal to survive at a subsistence level. Arguably the biggest losers in the new scheme of things were the landless agricultural wage-workers, whose numbers swelled by 60 percent between 1940 and 1960, and who accounted for half of the agricultural workforce, though they accounted for only 8 percent of agricultural income. Even in the prosperous agricultural zones, three quarters of landless families made less than $5 a month; a third got around $3.50 a month. It was not even a "subsistence" wage. The wage laborers had no job security, and were forced to pick up work whenever and wherever they could, often moving about to follow seasonal crops; they received no legal protection, got no social security or medical care, and had no access to adequate housing or education for their children.

As time passed, the position of all those at the bottom of the heap tended to deteriorate, largely because there were always more of them. One of Mexico's most pressing problems between 1930 and 1980 was its fantastically high rate of population increase. Prior to the 1970s the Mexican government saw population growth as a sign of economic health, and encouraged Mexicans to have large families. In the early 1940s Mexico had a total of about 20 million inhabitants. It added another 15 million by 1960, and by the mid-1960s its rate of population growth had hit 3.4 percent, the highest in the world. There was clearly not sufficient land to accommodate all of these new people. Even though Mexico's agricultural productivity soared during the 1950s and 1960s, it could not keep pace with the increase in population, so that the buying power of rural people declined by some 6 percent between 1940 and 1960. Much of the grain grown on the large northern farms was exported to more prosperous nations. Hunger and malnutrition remained serious problems, even in the midst of plenty.

The sins of the Mexican regime – and its international collaborators – did not lie only in its failure to recognize the hazards of runaway population growth. More damning still was the regime's stubborn adhesion to a model of economic development that was designed to increase the volume of production rather than the number of jobs. Green Revolution technologies aimed to save labor rather than to use it, so that the numbers of landless workers employed on large farms decreased even as the population exploded. Mexican development planners aggressively pursued industrial growth with a spate of policies known as "Import Substitution Industrialization." But industry grew haltingly, and it was plagued with many serious structural problems. Even though Mexico's industrial output increased fivefold between 1940 and 1965, that growth was outstripped by the growth in massive foreign borrowing and imports of technical goods and replacement parts, mostly from the United States. Industrial growth slowed further with respect to capital goods imports after 1965, by which time a crisis was well within sight and Mexico's "miracle" was fading. The focus on capital-intensive, rather than labor-intensive, growth meant that industry could absorb only a small fraction of the ever-growing population.

It almost seemed as though Mexico had entered the business of producing emigrants.

Managing Migration: The Bracero Program

The burgeoning supply of poor, unskilled, unemployed, desperate Mexicans was good news to American agribusiness. At the start of World

War II, the big growers once again painted an alarming picture of what would happen if they could not secure large quantities of cheap labor in short order – "entire crops being lost, the price of food doubling, banks closing, canneries going bankrupt, family farming ruined, and communism erupting in Mexico."[1] And, as had been the case during World War I, the growers were able to cast themselves as super patriots, for winning the war, and hence US national security, depended on the nation's production of adequate food and fiber.

Critics have raised credible doubts regarding the growers' assertions that they could find no domestic workers to pick their crops. But agriculture, with its inescapable seasonal imperatives, tends to create a permanent crisis mentality: if the crops are not picked in a timely fashion, they will be lost, and if there are not sufficient workers at the precise time of the year when the crops ripen, then those crops will not get picked. For the growers, a merely adequate supply of workers was not sufficient: there must be more workers than were, strictly speaking, needed. Workers who were in short or merely adequate supply might realize that they had leverage, and should they attempt to exercise that leverage, all could be lost. Of course, excess labor also ensured that wages would always remain low.

A large pool of surplus labor had another advantage that accrued only to large farmers: if growers could secure abundant labor at the start of the harvest, they could rush their produce onto the market, depressing prices and eventually driving small farmers – their competitors – into bankruptcy. These realities – together with that other annoyingly uncontrollable variable, the weather – kept farmers in a state of perpetual anxiety, their need for more and more workers a constant refrain. That much would be demonstrated when, as the crisis of world war wound down, the growers' loudly complained that their own crisis was ongoing.

America's entry into World War II did create problems. Millions of citizens were conscripted; the Japanese and Japanese Americans on the West Coast were rounded up and interned in concentration camps; many workers in the Southwest found higher paying farm jobs in Oregon and Washington; shipbuilding, aircraft manufacture, steel, and oil refining, all lured workers away from the fields. Those workers who were left were scarce enough to drive up wages, threatening even to provoke a bidding war among desperate growers. Growers panicked, for they feared that if they raised wages in order to cope with the generalized emergency of world war, those higher wages would become fixed and irremediable after the war was over. After all, growers had worked for decades to create a large, malleable, and mobile pool of workers, often using extreme brutality to keep wages as low as possible; they were loath to see that achievement undone by war.

Mexico seemed to provide the ideal solution to this problem, so long as Mexican workers could be properly managed. Mexicans were accustomed to working for low wages and in miserable conditions; they were ethnically and linguistically distinct from the majority population, and their homeland was close enough that they were unlikely to put down roots and try to blend in. If they made trouble, they could easily be returned to Mexico. Better yet, if Mexicans came to work in the United States as part of a contract labor program, they would be bound by their contracts and could not be seduced by higher paying industrial jobs; their numbers could be carefully controlled, so they would never be too many or too few; it was unlikely that they would be organized into labor unions; and, perhaps best of all, there was a good chance that the federal government, with national security concerns at the forefront, could be persuaded to subsidize the launching and maintenance of the program. If farmers could maintain wages at their customary low levels during wartime, it would be a major achievement. Moreover, many growers had long since come to think of access to cheap Mexican labor as an absolute right, so much so that they had often willfully violated laws that impinged upon that right.

The Bracero Program emerged out of these considerations.

Growers of cotton and sugar beets in California, New Mexico, Arizona, and Texas began requesting government help in recruiting labor from Mexico in early 1941, nearly a year before the Japanese attack on Pearl Harbor. Their requests were at first rejected, but in early 1942 they were heard with greater sympathy. Democratic Representative John H. Tolan of California took the lead in suggesting a joint program between the United States and Mexico to provide contracted labor to American farms and railroads.

The decision was not taken lightly, for despite the brief experiment with contracted labor during World War I, the use of foreign contract labor was traditionally viewed with great skepticism, at least in official circles, and it had been formally prohibited since 1885. Workers under contract were not free to seek other employment, negotiate for better pay and conditions, or quit their jobs. Their similarity to slaves or indentured servants was a bit too close for comfort. The labor union movement, which had fought for decades for the right to bargain collectively, vehemently opposed the notion of contract labor for the very reason that contract workers were not free. And although the labor movement would remain profoundly uncomfortable with the idea, US politicians, many of whom were themselves in thrall to the powerful farm bloc, saw real advantages in a contract labor program. It would ensure the harvests of southwestern crops, even while it allowed Mexico a chance to demonstrate its support for the war effort, Mexico having declared war on the Axis in June 1942.

Mexico had serious reservations about the program from the outset. There was still much anger in Mexico about the mass deportations of the 1930s, which had caused much hardship for many Mexicans. Elements within the United States had recently rattled sabers in response to Mexico's sweeping land reform and its 1938 oil expropriation, and Mexicans were understandably sensitive to US saber rattling. And reports of abuse of, and discrimination against, Mexican workers in the United States had long since become a staple of Mexican press reports.

Complicating the issue further, during the early 1940s Mexico was experiencing a rare outburst of optimism, a sense that its glittering industrial future was imminent and that soon Mexico would take its rightful place as "developed" nation and a major player on the world stage. The oil expropriation had seemed to make this vision plausible, since Mexico had defied its mighty neighbor and bested it in subsequent negotiations. Proud Mexicans saw no reason why Mexico should be perpetually cast in the role of mere adjunct to the United States economy, a supplier of stoop labor to those vast corporate farms of El Norte.

Still, Mexican officials recognized the potential benefits of a contract labor program. It would provide jobs for Mexico's numerous unemployed, taking some pressure off the regime's economic development projects; it would provide badly needed income in the form of remittances from those working in the United States; and it might even enhance Mexico's international prestige. In the past, Mexico had often enough approached the United States, hat in hand, seeking loans and investments and diplomatic recognition. This time, however, it was the United States that had come courting Mexico. The task of selling the program to the Mexican people was a bit delicate, but officials chose to emphasize that Mexico's participation would contribute vitally to the war against the Axis powers, even while allowing workers to learn new skills and technologies that would one day be used to modernize Mexico's own economy. And, assuming Mexico was able to drive a decent bargain, it could demand special protections for its workers, assuring them and their homeland of the respect and consideration that was their due. Mexico would be an equal partner with the United States in this undertaking.

Preliminary meetings were held in the spring of 1942. Mexico was anxious to maintain good relations with the United States, but, given the US labor shortage and the political pressure brought by farm interests, its bargaining power was considerable, and it was determined to use that power to good effect. To be sure, the Mexican government could be highly tolerant of the abuse of Mexicans within Mexico, so the hard line it took was at least partly for show: Mexico City newspapers showed great skepticism toward the program, and public opinion would have to be courted.

The agreement that emerged from the discussions in the spring of 1942 was tough enough. All recruitment was to be based on written contracts, and both the US and Mexican governments were to be responsible for guaranteeing those contracts. Before *braceros* could be recruited, it must be proved that a genuine need for workers existed, to ensure that *braceros* would never be used to lower wages or displace US domestic workers; *braceros* were not to be drafted into the US military, nor were they to be offered enticements to remain in the United States; either employers or the US government would have to provide transportation from the recruitment center in Mexico to the eventual work site, provide living expenses while en route, and bear the costs of repatriation at the termination of the contract period; housing and sanitation conditions had to be adequate, work must be guaranteed for at least three quarters of the duration of the contract, and wages were to be equal to the prevailing wage in a given area of employment, but never less than 30 cents per hour. Racial discrimination would not be tolerated, and Mexico reserved the right to deny *braceros* to any state or region that mistreated Mexicans.

Mexico's leverage would never be greater than it was during these initial negotiating sessions, and although it gained a bit with the labor shortages brought on by the Korean War in the early 1950s, as a general proposition its position weakened the longer the program persisted.

In the minds of its architects, the Bracero Program had three main objectives. They were (1) to ensure growers and railroad interests of a reliable source of labor for the duration of the wartime emergency (although the largest contingent of *braceros* was destined for the fields, about 80,000 worked in track maintenance for the railroads during the war years); (2) to protect the rights of Mexican "guest workers"; and (3) to eliminate the need for, and thus curtail, illegal immigration.

From the start, this was merely a fantasy of social engineering, its real chances of success virtually nil. It was doomed by a harsh reality: 30 cents an hour was hardly a handsome wage by US standards, but a farm worker in Mexico earned, on average, 6–8 cents an hour, with no guarantees of good housing or food or medical care – and that, of course, only for those lucky enough to find employment. The Bracero Program proved immediately attractive to millions of unemployed and underemployed rural Mexicans, so much so that, even before the agreement was formally announced, rumors, and ads placed by US farmers, began drawing streams of Mexicans northward. By August, the border towns of Ciudad Juárez, Mexicali, and Tijuana were packed with hungry men seeking *bracero* contracts. Mexican officials, concerned that overcrowding at the border would strain the resources of border towns, and fearful that the red tape involved in securing a contract might tempt migrants to slip across the border illegally, announced that recruiting would only be done in Mexico City. Predictably enough, soon Mexico City was inundated with some 50,000 aspiring *braceros*, most of them destitute and adding to the burdens of a city already teeming with poor people. Meanwhile, many of those who had gone to the border slipped illegally into the United States. American employers wanted to see recruiting done close to the border, since they were responsible for round-trip transportation of *braceros* and were eager to brighten their bottom line by passing as much as possible of that cost off to the migrants themselves. Soon enough, Mexico relented somewhat, opening contracting centers in several cities of the north-central region.

The immediate and immense popularity of the Bracero Program among poor Mexicans practically ensured that abuses would occur. And sure enough, abuses were soon widespread on both sides of the border. Some of those abuses became immediately apparent, others grew more pronounced as the program grew more prolonged and Mexico's bargaining power waned.

From the start, it was apparent that there was a problem with the agreement's insistence that *braceros* receive the "prevailing wage" for the region where they were employed. American growers continued to do as they had traditionally done, that is, meet in their associations prior to each harvest and decide what the "prevailing wage" would be. Naturally, the "prevailing wage" had to be low enough to ensure that it would not attract domestic workers, thereby ensuring the sort of labor "shortage" that was a prerequisite to obtaining *braceros*. Although the terms of the agreement specified that *braceros* were never to be used to displace domestic workers or to depress wages for farm work, practically every study ever done on the matter concluded that these were precisely the effects of *bracero* use.

Another problem arose with Mexico's efforts to defend its citizens working in the United States. Mexican officials concluded that their nationals were not well treated in the state of Texas, and in 1943 they made good on the threat to blacklist that state, citing "the number of cases of extreme, intolerable racial discrimination."[2] Texas Governor Coke Stevenson reacted energetically by appointing a six-member Good Neighbor Commission to look into and resolve problems involving discrimination against Mexicans and Mexican Americans. He took a goodwill tour of Mexico, assuring Mexicans that they could expect good treatment in Texas. Mexican Foreign Minister Ezequiel Padilla insisted that propaganda would not be a sufficient remedy, that tough laws and stiff penalties must be put in place for abuses against Mexicans. Governor Stevenson responded by immediately appointing a commission to study the enforcement issue, but even so, the evil reputation that Texas had acquired over the years ensured that the ban would remain in force until 1949, by which time Mexico's bargaining power was pretty well spent.

Still another problem arose with an agreement that brought some 80,000 Mexicans to the United States to perform track maintenance for the Southern Pacific, Santa Fe, and Western Pacific railroads. The

Figure 3.1   Aspiring *braceros* vie for contracts in Mexico City, 1945. Archivo General de la Nación, Fondo Hermanos Mayo.

contract for railroad workers was negotiated separately from that for agricultural workers. When it expired in August 1945, the railroad companies complained that their need for workers had not expired, and they refused to repatriate their workers as the agreement demanded. Those workers were practically held hostage until April 1946, and the matter provoked many complaints from the workers, the AFL, and the Mexican government. From that point on, *braceros* worked exclusively in agriculture.

The end of World War II presumably brought an end to the critical labor shortages, and the initial *bracero* agreement formally expired in 1947. But the growers were unwilling to see the program lapse. As one grower explained, "We are asking for labor only at certain times of the year – at the peak of our harvest – and the class of labor we want is the kind we can send home when we get through with them."[3] Accordingly, the growers lobbied hard for the continuance of the program beyond the war years, conjuring new and imaginative arguments on its behalf. Domestic workers had had a taste of higher wartime wages, and growers could not afford to pay the kind of wages that might entice them back to the fields. And all those countries that had been devastated by war would surely need to buy food from the United States, so farm production would have to be increased.

The Mexican government was ambivalent on the matter. On the one hand, the *braceros* had sent generous quantities of their earnings back to their families in Mexico, and their remittances had become vital to the Mexican economy; and unemployment in Mexico remained high after the war, raising the age-old issue of what to do with the surplus population. On the other hand, many interest groups in Mexico had vehemently opposed the Bracero Program from the beginning. Political parties of both the Right and Left saw the United States as an evil imperialist nation bent on exploiting Mexicans for its own ends. At the base of many of the criticisms of the program was the charge that Mexico's government, which continued to bill itself as "revolutionary," was manifestly unable to provide a decent livelihood for a large portion of Mexico's citizens.

But in some ways, Mexico's wishes had become practically irrelevant. After the war, Mexican *braceros* were more a luxury than a dire necessity for US employers, largely because of the tremendous influx of illegal immigrants. The United States made clear, starting in earnest in 1948, that it was resolved to press its advantages as the Bracero Program went forward.

A crisis began to build in early 1948, when Texas growers met and decided that the "prevailing wage" for cotton pickers would be $2.50 per hundred pounds picked. The Department of Labor, which inherited responsibility for the Bracero Program from the War Manpower Commission in early 1948, accepted the growers' proposed wage without carrying out a survey to determine if that wage was fair or reasonable. Mexican officials decided to take a stand, insisting that the wage be set at $3 per hundredweight. Texas growers were furious that anyone from outside their own circles should presume to dictate the wages they would pay. With the connivance of US Department of Labor officials, they caused rumors to circulate south of the border that cotton-picking jobs were to be had at $2.50 per hundredweight, but any takers had better hurry since the Mexican government intended to close the border. In response, between October 13 and 18, some 6,000 Mexican workers waded across the Rio Grande into the welcoming arms of the US Border

Patrol, which promptly "arrested" them and immediately "paroled" them to various south Texas cotton growers. Soon the labor glut in south Texas had driven the wage down to $1.50.

Mexican officials were outraged, threatening to abrogate the *bracero* agreement and to present the United States with claims on behalf of Mexican cotton growers, whose labor had been "seduced" by this patently illegal action. The United States quickly admitted that its actions were indeed illegal, apologized, and resumed negotiations for another *bracero* agreement (the agreement was renegotiated in 1947, 1948, and 1949). The immediate crisis was papered over, but after 1948 the Bracero Program assumed a starkly different character than it had had during the war years.

One of the most conspicuous features of the new, postwar order of things was a sharp rise in illegal immigration. In 1943, at the start of the program, the number of illegal immigrants deported was 8,860; by 1953 the figure had risen to 885,587. The Bracero Program, far from achieving the goal of stemming the tide of illegal immigration, was a major reason for the increase. This was largely the consequence of deliberate US policy.

In the United States, views of illegal immigration were equivocal. Southwestern employers saw some distinct advantages to undocumented workers. Undocumented workers were not covered by all of those annoying provisions stipulating minimum wages, decent housing, healthcare, and so forth, which many employers denounced as "socialistic." The downside was that, unlike *braceros*, illegal immigrants were free agents who were not bound by the "prevailing wage." If they should find themselves with a measure of bargaining power, they were free to make the most of it, and growers soon realized that undocumented workers could pick up stakes to chase rumors of higher wages, or that neighboring growers might pirate workers with offers of better pay.

In south Texas, where illegal immigrants were abundant, they could be, and were, exploited ruthlessly, but in other areas undocumented immigrants gained a reputation for being unreliable. The growers' preferred strategy was to field a mixed force of workers, with *braceros* and illegal immigrants balancing each other out, ensuring that workers would always be in abundant supply and making it improbable that they would be able to bargain for better pay. Using a mixed workforce of legal and illegal workers also had the advantage of allowing employers to demonstrate to the government that they were not dependent on the Bracero Program, so if the government got too enthusiastic about enforcing the many protections they were supposedly obligated to accord to *braceros*, employers could call its bluff with the assurance that, if the Bracero Program disappeared, they could always get the job done with illegal immigrants. Employers, of course, claimed not to know the legal status of their workers, but in most cases that was transparently false. There were notorious cases of especially unscrupulous employers calling in the Border Patrol at the end of the harvest, having agents round up and deport illegal immigrants just before payday.

The obstacles to illegal entry from Mexico had never been especially formidable. Informal border crossing was not made a crime until 1929, and after that the law was enforced only sporadically. As late as 1954, when illegal entry was approaching flood stage, the Border Patrol was able to field only about 200 patrolmen at any given time – clearly a number insufficient to provide anything more than token deterrence – and US Congressmen from the border states routinely sought to cut the agency's funding further still. Deportation of illegal immigrants, before it was streamlined in the 1950s, was a complicated matter, involving warrants and hearings that could take several days, during which time the immigrants had to be housed and fed. That presented a problem, since before 1945 there were no detention facilities on the border, and the facility at El Centro, California, which was completed in 1945, had space for only 200 detainees. Border Patrol agents, accordingly, only arrested as many illegal crossers as could be accommodated at any given time. And beyond that, a culture of disregard for the law had long since prevailed in matters involving immigration from Mexico. At harvest time, growers happily flouted the law by leaning on Border Patrol agents to relax their vigilance, and many growers declared that any interference by the government in their free use of illegal immigrants was un-American.

The Bracero Program increased illegal immigration in several ways. Perhaps most obviously, it allowed several millions of Mexicans to experience life in the United States and to achieve a level of familiarity and comfort there, perhaps learning a bit of English. They also managed to make contact with employers who made it clear that they would be happy to rehire them if, once their *bracero* contract was up, they should return to the United States illegally. Some immigrants presumably acquired tastes that were impossible to satisfy on the wages paid in Mexico, providing them a powerful incentive to return after their stints as *braceros* ended.

The Mexican blacklisting of Texas until 1949 gave illegal immigration a tremendous boost in that state. US officials sympathized with the Texas growers who were deprived of *braceros*, and tended to wink at violations of the immigration laws. Use of illegal immigrants was already part of the culture of south Texas, and it became even more ingrained as a result of the Bracero Program.

The massing of Mexicans near the northern border proved to be another spur to illegal entry. Although Mexico protested strenuously against locating contracting centers close to the border, it eventually lost that argument, and contracting centers were established in Monterrey, Chihuahua, Hermosillo, and Mexicali. Just as Mexican officials had feared, many workers who arrived at those contracting centers lost patience with the slow process and high cost of securing a *bracero* contract, and opted for the quicker, cheaper option of crossing into the United States *sans* documents.

In fact, *bracero* contracts were not easy to obtain, for there was plenty of red tape and the entire system was plagued by massive corruption. A would-be *bracero* had first to obtain a clearance from his town mayor (*presidente municipal*), a service for which some mayors charged fees that tended to rise as competition for contracts grew stiffer. If an aspiring *bracero* was eligible for the military draft, he might have to pay a bribe to the military inspector; he then had to pay for transportation to the contracting center; and once there he was usually liable for a fee of about $50, though roguish officials often made would-be *braceros* shell out much more. In all, many Mexican jobseekers found that it was much cheaper and quicker to pay a smuggler to help them enter the United States illegally.

The United States also contributed mightily to the influx of undocumented workers as a matter of deliberate policy. Especially conducive to increasing illegal immigration was a practice that came to be known as "drying out the wetbacks." This practice grew out of ongoing, and generally fruitless, discussions between the United States and Mexico in which each accused the other of not doing enough to prevent illegal migration. At one such meeting in the spring of 1944, Mexican delegates promised to urge their government to adopt measures to curb illegal migration – in fact, the Mexican government would do very little in this regard – while the US representatives promised to carry out an immediate program of repatriation of illegal migrants. Between June and December 1944 the United States apprehended and deported about 45,000 illegal migrants, which not only antagonized some American growers who relied on that labor, but it also caused severe crowding problems in the border towns of Tijuana and Mexicali – towns that were virtually unconnected to the rest of Mexico by road or rail, and that did not have the wherewithal to care for the sudden influx of deportees. Mexico pleaded with the United States to return deportees through the more conveniently located ports of Juárez or Nuevo Laredo, but the United States deemed that to be excessively expensive.

So, in the hope of avoiding congestion at the border and a perpetual pattern of border jumping by the recently deported, negotiators hit upon the solution of simply legalizing the illegals. Mexico was on board with the idea, based on the assumption that legally contracted workers would have assurances of better treatment than illegal migrants. Accordingly, a protocol was signed in early 1947 providing for the return of 100,000 illegal immigrants through the ports of Mexicali, Juárez, and Reynosa, where they would be immediately processed for legal re-entry as *braceros*. The agreement mandated that any employers who continued to use illegal workers after this were to be barred from the program, and there was also a strong suggestion by the Mexican negotiators that the United States should impose serious penalties on the employers of illegal immigrants. The United States, fearful of antagonizing the powerful farm bloc, generally ignored those details, but the "drying out" program got underway immediately, and in short order the vast majority of *braceros* working in the United States were in fact former "wetbacks" who had undergone the "drying out" process.

In California the "drying out" process soon became practically ritualized. Contractors would load buses full of illegal immigrants from various ranches and farms and spirit them off to Calexico. There, consuls at the US immigration post would certify the migrants and make them touch one foot on south-of-the-border soil; then the migrants would

Figure 3.2   During the 1950s the United States allowed undocumented Mexican workers to set one foot on Mexican soil in order to "re-enter" the country legally with a *bracero* contract. The process was known as "drying out the wetbacks." Photo by Loomis Dean/Time Life Pictures/Getty Images.

"re-enter" the United States, miraculously cleansed of all transgression. An agreement hashed out in 1949 decreed that Mexicans already working illegally in the United States were to be "given preference for employment under outstanding United States Employment Service certification."[4] Mexican officials pointed out that this policy would likely tempt Mexicans to enter the United States illegally in the hope of being rewarded with a *bracero* contract. US officials therefore decreed that no worker could receive a *bracero* contract unless he had been in the United States for at least three months. That provision proved no obstacle: aspiring *braceros* could simply lie about the amount of time they had been in the United States. During fiscal year 1950, fewer than 20,000 new *braceros* got contracts, while nearly 97,000 "wetbacks" were "dried out." "Dried out wetbacks" continued to outnumber new recruits for the remainder of the program's existence.

In 1950 Mexico found its bargaining power temporarily increased as a result of US entry into the Korean War, which once again inspired growers to complain of a labor shortage. Mexico was not shy about voicing its concerns about the deterioration of the Bracero Program since the end of World War II. As of 1947, the US government refused to act as the formal employer of *braceros*, allowing instead for contracting directly between workers and employers. That had the predictable effect of permitting employers to abuse the program's provisions with relative impunity, and abuses – sometimes apocryphal – were given ample play in the Mexican press. A US presidential commission on migratory labor chimed in with a report that slammed the Bracero Program for depressing wages, displacing domestic workers, and encouraging illegal immigration.

Mexico made the most of its fleeting leverage, refusing to renew the Bracero Program if the United States did not guarantee compliance with preconditions and penalize employers of illegal immigrants. The result of these negotiations was Public Law 78 (PL 78), passed in 1951, which restated all of the requirements of the original program, made the US Secretary of Labor responsible for enforcement, and instituted contracting fees of between $3 and $15 that growers would have to pay for each *bracero* they employed. The law also included provisions for "drying out wetbacks," allowing individuals with over five years in the United States to be placed under contract. Labor unions, human rights groups, and Mexican-American organizations criticized the law, calling for much stronger protections, including a guaranteed minimum wage, public hearings to certify shortages of labor, and guarantees that domestic workers would receive the same benefits promised to *braceros*.

The Bracero Program would be governed by PL 78 till its end in 1964, though during the mid- to late-1950s growers – with the help of their Congressional allies, mostly Republicans from rural districts – enjoyed great success in weakening enforcement of the agreement's provisions.

High Tensions and "Operation Wetback"

The year 1954 was pivotal for the fate of the Bracero Program, for it witnessed one serious international incident and one program of mass deportation. The international incident was precipitated by the fact that PL 78 was set to expire at the end of 1953, and Mexican officials thought they saw an opportunity to make some improvements. Although generally in favor of continuing the Bracero Program, Mexican leaders were sensitive to criticism of the program's flaws. The 1951 agreement had insisted that the United States impose penalties on the employers of illegal immigrants, but legislation that the United States enacted in 1952 – known as the McCarran-Walter Act – only made it a felony to "import" or "harbor" an illegal alien. Democratic Senator Paul Douglas of Illinois proposed an amendment that would have made it a felony to employ a known or suspected illegal immigrant, but that proposal was overwhelmingly defeated. Pressure from Texas lawmakers resulted in the inclusion of the so-called "Texas Proviso," which said explicitly that employing did not constitute "importing" or "harboring." The Act added insult to injury by barring communists or other subversives from migrating to the United States, a provision that allowed the Immigration Service to prevent known or suspected Mexican labor organizers from crossing the border, and to deport any that were already in the country. This allowed the government's critics – most notably, leftist labor leader Vicente Lombardo Toledano, who ran for president in 1952 – to paint the Bracero Program as a boon to American employers that was riddled with corruption, exploitation, and racism.

In addition to persuading the United States to impose sanctions on the employers of illegal immigrants, Mexican negotiators hoped to secure for Mexico greater leverage in determining the wages that *braceros* would be paid. The Mexicans hoped their cause might be helped by the fact that the United States' relations with Latin America had deteriorated badly since the end of World War II, owing mostly to the growing US obsession with international communism. A show of good neighborliness might, they apparently reasoned, have a salutary effect on those relations.

The Mexicans clearly overestimated their own influence, and underestimated the strength of US commercial farmers. The United States flatly refused the Mexican demands. The Mexicans then reluctantly agreed to extend the old agreement till January 15, 1954, but refused to negotiate a new one on US terms. The US Departments of Labor, State, and Justice, at that point, issued a press release saying that the United States would begin recruiting *braceros* unilaterally, without the acquiescence of the Mexican government. Once apprised of this news, impoverished Mexicans began flocking to the northern border by the thousands, till the border towns were choked with hungry, homeless men, and a crisis seemed imminent. Mexico declared that no one would be allowed to cross the border, and that any who managed to do so would face punishment.

By the time Mexico dispatched armed troops to the border, about 700 people had already entered the United States. US officials ramped up the tension by announcing that any Mexicans who managed to cross the border would be contracted as *braceros,* their only obligation being to step one foot onto Mexican soil so they could then "re-enter" the country free of taint.

The presence of so many desperate people in Mexico's northern border towns raised tensions and on occasion took violent turns. In Mexicali about 500 men marched on the palace of Baja California Governor Braulio Maldonado demanding food and jobs, only to be dispersed by soldiers with fire hoses. The governor then tried to placate the men by offering them free transportation home, but there were few takers.

On January 22, Border Patrol agents at several border crossings opened the gates and invited the crowds to enter. What followed was a scene of predictable pandemonium: at several towns along the boundary, Border Patrol agents tried to pull migrants across the border while Mexican soldiers sought to prevent their crossing or to pull them back south. Mexican troops used water hoses, guns, clubs, and whatever else they could grab, but they were overrun.

Both US and Mexican officials were alarmed by the violence. Mexico backed down, now declaring that no one would be impeded from crossing into the United States, while the United States declared that it would institute an interim program to bring some order to the chaos at the border.

But still, chaos reigned. This time, it was US officials trying to hold back the throngs with a human chain, squad cars, and fire hoses. But like their Mexican counterparts, they proved no match for the advancing multitude. Efforts to contain the flow by offering limited numbers of contracts only made matters worse. At Calexico the 500 contracts offered on February 1 were gone in 20 minutes, and the 8,000–10,000 men who failed to get contracts charged the gate, braving fire hoses and tear gas.

Some were successfully turned back, but most of them broke through during a few days in early February.

Although both US and Mexican officials tried to paint the rosiest possible face on these events, assuring each other and their respective publics that it was nothing that could not be resolved happily within the bounds of good neighborliness, the 1954 border episode was pivotal. It was one among several episodes from the early 1950s that severely soured relations between the United States and Latin America. The United States made clear that it did not intend to be hamstrung by any need to defer to the world's less powerful nations. As one State Department official put it bluntly, in contrast to the years of World War II, "the United States no longer desperately needs Latin America."[5] By mid-February the Eisenhower administration announced it would resume negotiations with Mexico for a new *bracero* agreement, and indeed a new agreement was signed on March 10. But a few days later the United States amended a clause from Section 501 of PL 78, replacing the phrase "pursuant to arrangements between the United States and the Republic of Mexico" with the phrase "pursuant to arrangements between the United States and the Republic of Mexico or after every practicable effort has been made by the United States to negotiate and reach agreement on such arrangement."[6] The United States made sure to reserve for itself the right to act unilaterally if it could not get its way through diplomacy.

Mexican officials were understandably shocked and outraged by US arrogance. There is little doubt that US actions in this episode were patently illegal and, in the words of one California Congressman, they "ignored every consideration of human decency, international courtesy, and, in short, everything but the demands of the organized growers bent on an open door to cheap farm labor, regardless of the consequences."[7] But it was dawning on Mexican officials that there was not much they could do about it. From 1954 onward, despite a handful of minor, almost cosmetic, reforms, PL 78 would remain unchanged, and Mexico's bargaining power in the matter was virtually nil.

Perhaps more humiliating for the Mexican government, however, was the spectacle of so many of Mexico's citizens displaying their desperation by traveling hundreds of miles, braving violence and hardship, and risking death, merely to secure the most menial jobs the United States had to offer. Since the Mexican Revolution, the Mexican government had

Figure 3.3 Many Mexicans who were unable to get *bracero* contracts entered the United States illegally. In this photo from 1950, undocumented workers gather at Ciudad Juárez, Chihuahua, waiting for a chance to cross. Archivo General de la Nación, Fondo Hermanos Mayo.

made much of the concept of a "Mexican family," of which the government was cast as the stern but caring patriarch. For years the regime had sought to portray itself as bringing modernity and prosperity to its citizens. Many middle-class Mexicans, sheltered from the country's grim realities, were shocked to learn how forlorn so many of their countrymen were. The Mexican government likely paid a price for this, though it was just one of many events that were progressively eroding popular trust.

The curious and contradictory policies pursued by the United States did not stop with its unilateral recruitment of *braceros*. The ironies and contradictions in the Bracero Program were striking indeed. Originally billed as a supplement to domestic labor, which would help to curb illegal immigration from Mexico, in fact by the mid-1950s Mexican workers had displaced domestic workers in many areas, and the Bracero Program was itself little more than a supplement to illegal immigration. When Americans began to realize that the majority of Mexican laborers in the

United States were in the country illegally, they reacted with something bordering on hysteria. Many Americans were soon calling noisily for expulsion. Out of this hysteria was born the bizarre policy of the mid-1950s: enticing people to enter the country illegally, on the one hand; and on the other hand, plotting a wholesale round up and deportation of "wetbacks."

Hostility toward the "wetbacks" was at least in part a function of race prejudice, something that was hardly new in the United States. Resentment of Mexicans had been growing fairly steadily since the 1920s. During the 1930s it was ascribed to competition for scarce jobs, but it continued on into the 1940s, exploding in 1943 in the notorious "Zoot Suit Riots," when US servicemen in Los Angeles went on a rampage, beating and intimidating Mexicans and Mexican Americans throughout the city. By the early 1950s, in a development that likely had much to do with rising Cold War paranoia, Americans began heaping scorn on undocumented Mexicans. One immigration official famously denounced the influx of illegal immigrants as "the greatest peacetime invasion ever complacently suffered by another country under open, contemptuous, flagrant violations of its laws."[8] The President's Commission on Migratory Labor in 1951 declared that illegal immigrants did indeed lower wages and displace domestic workers, something that came as unwelcome news during the economic recession of the early 1950s and inspired organized labor once again to demand curbs on immigration. Soon enough, newspapers and magazines were filled with articles painting illegal immigrants as alien invaders bent on undermining the American way of life. Those immigrants were charged with carrying loathsome diseases, having unalterable criminal proclivities, burdening welfare, debasing morality, and thinking subversive thoughts. Words like "horde," "tide," "flood," and "invasion" became standard fare in discussions of the topic.

For the most part, undocumented immigrants were unorganized and illiterate. They were in no condition to advocate for themselves, and practically no one was willing to advocate on their behalf. And those immigrants had plenty to complain about. Although the penalties for illegal entry were light, the experience was hard and perilous. Coyotes might charge $50, and many were unscrupulous or unreliable. Migrants suffered and sometimes died from thirst, exposure, or starvation while attempting to cross the harsh terrain; they risked snakebites and gunshots. In 1953 alone, some 400 people drowned trying to swim flood-swollen rivers. At parts of the border migrants had to find ways to get through barbed wire fences. Enterprising individuals might cut holes in the fences with blowtorches and then charge others to go through those holes; others rented out mattresses that could be laid across the wire.

Once in the United States, undocumented immigrants had virtually no protections. Many lived in unspeakable conditions: makeshift tents or shacks without running water, sanitation facilities, or heat. Children of illegal immigrants suffered from malnutrition, dysentery, diarrhea, and other ailments. Employers often refused to acknowledge any responsibility toward illegal workers. Occupational safety was seldom a concern. Illegal immigrants suffered transportation accidents, were mangled by machinery, and breathed toxic chemicals. Wage theft was a problem, often done in connivance with law enforcement officers, who might round up workers for deportation at the end of the harvest, prior to payday. Some employers claimed that illegal immigrants made better workers than their *bracero* counterparts, though it is debatable whether they admired their gumption or their limitless exploitability. "Wetbacks" were especially popular in the lower Rio Grande Valley of Texas.

In 1953 the US economy slowed, and once again illegal immigrants made handy scapegoats. The issue suddenly took on the dimensions of a crisis, capturing the attention of Attorney General Herbert Brownell, who had earlier dismissed the matter as a distant priority. Brownell toured southern California in August, speaking to labor organizers, welfare workers, healthcare providers, clergy, and state employment officials, all of whom gave him an earful about the evils of illegal immigration. They charged that illegal immigrants were driving down wages, taking jobs from citizens, and putting a strain on police, hospital, and welfare budgets. Brownell also spoke to growers, who defended the illegal immigrants, complaining that *braceros* were too expensive and the procedures for securing them too complicated. But the critics of illegal immigration carried the day. Brownell set about addressing the problem with the zeal of a religious convert.

Brownell's first statement on the issue revealed a substantial increase in funding for the Border Patrol. Shortly thereafter, he suggested that legislation be sent to Congress to curb illegal entry. That proposed legislation, eventually passed as S.3660, called for the forfeiture of any vehicle or vessel used to transport illegal immigrants. It also addressed the employers of illegal immigrants, but in a manner that was altogether toothless. The law amounted to a mere suggestion that employers refrain from "knowingly" hiring illegal immigrants. It would have been quite difficult to prove that such hiring was done "knowingly," and even if it could be proved, the law imposed no criminal penalties on employers. Curiously, while the law did not actually ban the employing of illegal immigrants, it did outlaw the payment of money for services provided by illegal immigrants, giving cynical employers a handy excuse for wage theft. The law was clearly an attempt to placate public opinion – which was becoming increasingly hostile toward illegal immigrants – while not alienating the powerful farm bloc.

The second part of Brownell's initiative was more effective. This was a major undertaking known as "Operation Wetback," which was engineered by newly hired Commissioner of Immigration Joseph Swing. Swing was a highly decorated, retired Army lieutenant general who had studied with Dwight Eisenhower at West Point, joined General Pershing's effort to hunt down Mexican revolutionary Pancho Villa in 1916, and served with distinction in both world wars. Swing designed the operation as an almost military offensive, though the actual military declined to participate. Swing whipped the Border Patrol into fighting shape, retiring or transferring ineffective officers, and reorganizing the force to be more nimble and mobile. Twelve-man task forces were created, each with radio-equipped vehicles. The task forces were able to assemble "Special Mobile Forces" of several hundred men on short notice. They focused their efforts in areas known for their high concentrations of illegal immigrants. Swing announced at the start of June that the Border Patrol would begin a mass round up and deportation of undocumented Mexicans. Signs and billboards were erected with stern warnings in Spanish: "The Era of the Wetback and the Wire Cutter Has Ended! From This Day Forward Any Person Found in the United States Illegally Will be Punished by Imprisonment."[9] Tens of thousands fled to Mexico rather than await capture.

Operation Wetback had the full approval and cooperation of the Mexican government, which, though it continued to urge serious penalties for employers of illegal immigrants, was pleased that the United States at last appeared to be doing something to address the matter of illegal migration.

The operation was extremely unpopular among Texas farmers, so Swing selected California and Arizona as the first targets. Aircraft were used to detect the locations of illegal immigrants. Once detected, jeeps would sweep in and cordon off the targeted area, and the arrests would begin, with the detainees loaded onto trucks and taken to detention camps, eventually to be returned to Mexico by bus, train, or ship. By mid-June the task forces had surpassed General Swing's stated goal of 1,000 arrests per day. Mexico, while generally approving of the operation, soon found itself protesting the scale of the deportations, for it was poorly prepared to absorb so many people on such short notice.

The operation encountered considerable resistance in the lower Rio Grande Valley of Texas, where growers paid abysmally low wages to undocumented cotton pickers. South Texas growers had a long history of antagonism toward Border Patrol agents, deriding them as "goon squads," "the Gestapo," and an "army of occupation." Wives and children of Border Patrol agents were harassed and ostracized. The Border Patrol's antagonists got plenty of support from the local press, law enforcement, and even Texas Governor Allen Shivers, who himself employed illegal immigrants. Even so, the operation forged ahead, such that by late July nearly 42,000 Mexicans had been ousted from Texas and many more had left of their own accord.

In the end, the Immigration and Naturalization Service claimed that, between deportations and voluntary departures, 1,300,000 Mexicans had left the United States as a result of Operation Wetback, a figure that is likely exaggerated. The 1955 INS report pronounced the operation an unqualified success. "The so-called 'wetback' problem no longer exists," the report boasted. "The border has been secured."[10]

Naturally, Operation Wetback once again set growers to howling about the severe labor shortages they faced. To placate them, the government expanded and streamlined the Bracero Program. The numbers of *bracero* contracts granted grew from 201,280 in 1953 to a peak of 447,535 in 1959. To follow up on the successes of Operation Wetback, new intelligence agencies were created to study and obstruct illegal entry; new fences were erected or repaired near the larger border cities; and the Border Patrol, previously a neglected agency, now basked in glory, its funding increased for the next several years.

Claims that Operation Wetback was an unqualified success were overstated, to say the least. As historian Juan Ramón García points out, operations of this kind attacked symptoms, not causes.[11] The operation obviously did nothing to erase the enormous gap in wealth between the United States and Mexico, or to create good jobs in Mexico. In some ways, the operation worsened the situation. Even though during the second half of the 1950s and early 1960s, the majority of Mexicans living and working in the United States were legal, their working conditions deteriorated. In order to further appease growers riled by Operation Wetback, the government eased its regulation of the Bracero Program, and predictable abuses appeared. One grower described the situation candidly: "We used to buy our slaves; now we rent them from the Government."[12]

Workers lodged relatively few formal complaints, but that likely had much to do with the difficulties involved in the formal grievance process. Among themselves and to their consuls, *braceros* complained frequently of subminimum wages, unauthorized deductions from paychecks, food that often consisted of such fare as sheep heads and chicken necks and moldy leftovers, substandard housing, lack of job safety, and occasionally even physical abuse by employers.[13]

Defenders of the Bracero Program claimed that it greatly benefited individual Mexicans who participated, giving them the opportunity to earn wages far higher than those to which they were accustomed. Those defenders also maintained that the program helped Mexico, which received so much money in the form of *bracero* remittances that remittances became the country's second largest source of foreign exchange, after tourism. One estimate held that every *bracero* supported on average four people in Mexico, greatly easing the burden on the Mexican government to create jobs or provide welfare. There is evidence that some *braceros* acquired skills in the United States that later contributed to economic development in Mexico, but since the vast majority of *braceros* devoted themselves to stoop labor, that the impact was most likely modest. Some *braceros* were able to buy land, livestock, houses, and motor vehicles with the money they had saved. Anecdotal evidence suggests that the vast majority of *braceros* spoke well of their experiences in the United States, especially of their gratification at being able to earn eight to ten times what they would have earned in Mexico.

Still, as historian Luis González notes, "When everything is added up, it turns out that the *bracero* program took more than it gave."[14] It emptied many Mexican villages of their most enterprising citizens. By 1960, for instance, in the village of Tzintzuntzan, Michoacán, 50 percent of all adult males had been to the United States at least once, and several had been there up to ten times. Nearly all of them, according to an American anthropologist who worked in the village, allowed that they would like to go back again.[15] Travel to the United States for work had become "an accepted and expected life experience,"[16] one that separated families and inspired some men never to return home. Some remained in the United States, while many more were seduced by the relative glamour and sophistication of Mexico City, which metastasized alarmingly. The problem was that, even had the amounts of capital imported by *braceros* been sufficient to effect meaningful economic change, the Bracero Program was neither designed nor intended to uplift Mexico. American employers, who were the prime beneficiaries of the program, made wildly exaggerated claims about the program's effectiveness as international aid: it was not just a boon to the Mexican economy, they insisted, but it also instilled democracy and impeded the spread of communism. But unfortunately, neither the Mexican nor the US governments did anything to channel *bracero* income into the most productive areas, and as a result the lion's share of that income went toward the purchase of consumer goods: transistor radios, clothing, gadgets, and motor vehicles, most of US manufacture. The money sent home by *braceros* arguably helped Mexico to stave off a severe crisis in unemployment and hunger, but it had little lasting impact on the country's economic development.

Among the casualties of the Bracero Program were American farm workers. Virtually every serious study of the impact of the program found it failed dismally in fulfilling its initial goals. The program mandated that *braceros* were not to be used to displace domestic farm workers, yet they certainly did so. This is evidenced by the fact that, in some farming areas, 100 percent of the workforce was Mexican, even though *braceros* were supposed to merely supplement the domestic workforce. The program likewise mandated that *braceros* were not to depress wages or lessen the quality of life for rural workers, yet they seem to have done so. Farm wages in California remained stagnant for the entire decade of the 1950s, except in areas that saw the lightest use of *braceros*. One study contended that *braceros* caused farm wages to decrease by 8.8 percent per year.[17] Farm workers remained by far the lowest-paid workers in the country, earning on average one fifth what factory workers earned. And, in truly grotesque violation of both the spirit and letter of the law, in 1947 and again in 1951, *braceros* were trucked in to act as strikebreakers during cantaloupe pickers' strikes in California, and they were made to perform the same role in a 1950 tomato pickers' strike in San Joaquin county.

Undoubtedly the greatest beneficiaries of the program were precisely those individuals that the program was *intended* to benefit, namely large agribusiness interests, who represented only about 2 percent of all farmers in the United States. It gave them a major competitive edge against their rivals, such that the heyday of the Bracero Program coincided with a drastic decrease in the numbers of family farms. The total number of farms in California declined from 137,000 to 99,000 between 1950 and 1960, while total acreage under cultivation decreased by some 313,000 acres, most of the loss being sustained by farms under 500 acres. During that same decade, cotton farming was able to transition from a plantation system using massive numbers of sharecroppers and migrant pickers to a fully mechanized and modern farming system. Without the Bracero Program, it is likely that cotton farming would have faced a serious crisis, for from the 1940s onward it proved difficult to persuade domestic workers to pick cotton, even while substantial amounts of labor were required while the industry was in the process of mechanization. The Bracero Program helped to make that transition possible. By 1964, the last year of the Bracero Program, three quarters of American cotton was being harvested by machine. In the final analysis, the Bracero Program amounted to a massive government subsidy to powerful farming interests.

By the early 1960s, liberal Democrats were in the ascendancy in Washington. Those Democrats were closely tied to organized labor and also sympathetic to the plight of domestic farm workers, which made them harsh critics of the Bracero Program. They were helped in their efforts by a powerful television documentary, *Harvest of Shame*, in which journalist Edward R. Murrow exposed the plight of domestic, mostly African-American, migratory farm workers, bringing the deplorable conditions of migrant workers out from the shadows and into the national consciousness. While making it clear that they wished to do away with the program altogether, liberals began pushing through changes to the system, including an amendment requiring that farmers pay domestic workers the same wages, with the same hours and physical conditions, as were offered to *braceros* and limiting the areas in which *braceros* could be used. The liberals in Congress were joined by religious, labor, and human rights groups, who eventually proved stronger than coalitions of growers. In 1963 growers and their allies tried to get yet another two-year extension of the program, and Congress rejected that, opting instead for a one-year extension. When that extension ended at the end of 1964, the program was allowed to expire.

4

Illegal Immigration and Response

1964–1990

By the 1970s, Mexico's "miracle" of sustained economic growth appeared to be over as the country entered upon a prolonged series of shocks – violence, debt, inflation, mass unemployment – that increased the already robust demand among Mexicans for jobs in the United States. But as fate would have it, the Bracero Program was terminated at the very time the US Congress chose to undertake a sweeping reform of US immigration law, granting Mexico a quota of visas that was woefully inadequate to the demand among Mexicans desperate for work. The outcome was a predictable spike in the rates of undocumented immigration from Mexico, and a just as predictable rise in alarm among the American public. As had happened so often in the past, the immigration problem was seized upon by demagogues and made to seem more severe than it actually was. Against this backdrop, some members of Congress set themselves the unenviable task of trying to create an immovable object to confront this apparently unstoppable force. The result was a 1986 law that ended up having many ironic and unintended effects, one of which was yet another sharp spike in the volume of Mexican undocumented immigration to the United States.

Beyond Borders: A History of Mexican Migration to the United States
By Timothy J. Henderson
© 2011 Timothy J. Henderson

Crisis in Mexico

By the late 1960s, even while some observers continued to express awe at the "Mexican Miracle," the essential bankruptcy of the nation's development strategy had become glaringly apparent. That strategy was founded in the conviction that economic development, as conceived by the "classical" or "liberal" economic theory that had prevailed in the world's rich countries since before the industrial revolution of the 1700s, was fundamentally wrong. Classical economics suggested that each of the world's countries should focus its efforts on what nature had best equipped it to do. Those countries and regions that were by-passed by the first waves of industrial development were supposed to supply raw materials and to purchase the goods produced in the industrialized countries. By the third decade of the twentieth century, it was apparent to most in the non-industrialized world that the industrialized countries were holding all the best cards, and that those countries were enriching themselves at the expense of the poor ones. Accordingly, poorer countries hit upon a strategy to bring on an industrial revolution by force. Broadly labeled "Import Substitution Industrialization" (ISI), this strategy gave the state the dominant role in fomenting domestic industries that would produce goods that previously had been imported.

This strategy was a matter of general consensus in Mexico, though there was no universal agreement on the particulars. Mexico's revolutionary Constitution of 1917 had made the state a leading player in national affairs, but its language tended to suggest that state interventions would be geared toward bettering the lot of the peasants and working classes. The government of Lázaro Cárdenas had enacted policies that indicated that the benefits of industrialization might be widely shared. But from 1940 onward, the Mexican state instead chose to lavish blessings on economic elites, with the vague promise that sooner or later those blessings would trickle down to the masses. The state was to provide a variety of protections and incentives that would allow for the development of industry without the menace of foreign competition. Protective tariffs, import licensing, and currency manipulation would provide the needed protection, while tax incentives, subsidies, infrastructure development, and in some cases outright state ownership would give industries the wherewithal to get up and running.

In many ways this effort enjoyed remarkable success. During the 1960s Mexico's gross domestic product (GDP) grew at a rate of between 6 and 7 percent per year, the highest sustained rate of growth in Latin America. Between 1940 and 1970 industry's share of Mexico's GDP increased from less than 18 percent to 26 percent, though factories managed to employ only around 16 percent of the total workforce. Agriculture decreased its share of GDP from 23 percent to 16 percent, even while it employed slightly more than half of the total workforce. Neither industry nor agriculture was able to provide adequate employment opportunities for Mexicans. Foreign transnational corporations were active in Mexico also, but they did little to alleviate the problem. While foreign companies controlled 31 percent of the value of Mexican industrial production, they employed only 16 percent of the industrial workforce.

The spectacular industrialization that took place during the 1950s and 1960s tended to obscure the many problems inherent in the ISI strategy. The systematic underfunding of all but the most commercially viable agriculture added to the impoverishment of rural Mexico. United States-based transnational corporations like Del Monte and Anderson-Clayton came to dominate many of Mexico's most lucrative crops, such as cotton and winter vegetables, further marginalizing smaller farmers and most of the *ejidos*.

Meanwhile, the obsessive focus on developing infrastructure and industry left precious little revenue to invest in "social" expenditure: between 1935 and 1960, an average of less than 15 percent of yearly budgets was devoted to such matters as education, social security, health and welfare, housing, food, and subsidies for transportation. Expenditures of this kind rose only moderately during the 1960s. By the late 1950s Mexico was spending less of its revenues on education than any Latin American country. Aid to the rural poor was pitifully inadequate – by 1970 there was only one agricultural extension agent for every 10,000 farm families. By the late 1960s only 6 percent of Mexico's people were covered by social security benefits, although the social security law had been on the books since 1943. And, not surprisingly given these trends, by the 1960s the distribution of wealth in Mexico was among the most unequal in the world.

The notion that the poor might eventually come to share the wealth was far fetched. Given the low level of tax collection, much of the capital and technology used to jumpstart Mexico's industrial development was borrowed from overseas, meaning that the nation's debt burden increased gradually as the "miracle" progressed, creating further obstacles to any efforts to redistribute wealth. Those industries that did arise did so behind the protective shield imposed by the state; facing no competition from imports, and enjoying a captive market, they tended to produce shoddy, uncompetitive goods. But most damning to Mexico's long-term prospects was the fact that, given the extreme gap between rich and poor, and the appalling factor by which the latter outnumbered the former, there was scant possibility that a domestic market could develop that might make Mexico's industrial economy sustainable. Simply put, few Mexicans could afford to buy the goods their country produced, imposing an insuperable limit on just how far Mexico's economic "miracle" could go. Adding greatly to these structural defects was Mexico's rate of population growth, which remained staggeringly high. Until the early 1970s Mexican women were giving birth to an average of 6.5 children each, causing the population to mushroom from 26.3 million in 1950 to 69.7 million in 1980. There was little prospect that Mexico's economy, its "miraculous" character notwithstanding, could provide employment for so many new citizens.

This is the context in which the United States chose to terminate the Bracero Program. Mexican officials seem to have been fairly blindsided by the news, even though the end of the program had been telegraphed for years. The numbers of *bracero* contracts had been in decline since the highpoint in the late 1950s, when the United States was providing over 400,000 contracts per year. In 1964 it offered fewer than 200,000 contracts. Still, Mexico took the termination of the program seriously enough to agree to a US proposal to undertake a novel program aimed at providing employment in the border region. The Border Industrialization Program (BIP), as it was called, relaxed Mexican laws barring wholly owned subsidiaries of foreign corporations from setting up shop in the country. United States corporations located plants, known as *maquiladoras*, just south of the US border. Maquiladoras imported parts and supplies duty free, assembled those parts into finished garments, electronic devices, auto parts, furniture, and other goods, and then re-exported the finished products back to the United States. By 1980 there were 620 such plants employing 100,000 workers; by 1992 the number had grown to 2,000, employing over half a million workers; and at present, more than 3,000 maquiladoras, owned by a variety of multinational interests, employ more than a million workers.

Although since the 1990s the maquiladora sector has been gaining in sophistication, the early plants were classic "economic enclaves," that is, operations that principally served the interests of foreign companies while bringing only modest benefits to the host country. The maquiladoras provided poorly paid employment for some Mexicans living in the border region and some tax revenues to the state. However, most of their inputs were imported, so they did little to stimulate new industries in Mexico that might, for example, have provided machinery, parts, and raw materials to the plants. Moreover, the early maquiladoras did little to solve the unemployment problem, since those plants preferred to hire women and even children – people who had not previously participated in the labor market. There were some charges that the maquiladoras were counterproductive with respect to migration, since some who were drawn to the border region in search of maquiladora employment might, upon failing to find such jobs, take the next logical step across the border into the United States. Evidence for this hypothesis is far from conclusive; most researchers have found that the overall impact of maquiladoras on immigration has been negligible.[1]

By the late 1960s the giddy optimism of the postwar period was fading. In the autumn of 1968, as Mexico prepared to welcome the world to its capital for the summer Olympic games, a massive student movement took to the streets of Mexico City demanding greater democracy and openness. From the perspective of Mexico's ruling elites, it was as though the government was being threatened by one of its greatest success stories: middle-class city kids who had enjoyed the benefits of tuition-free college education and who should be looking forward to gainful employment in government and industry, now suddenly turned subversive. A series of violent crackdowns against the movement culminated on October 2 when troops and police opened fire on a demonstration held at the Plaza de Tlatelolco (also known as the Plaza of Three Cultures), killing and wounding an unknown number of protestors (the most common estimates range between 200 and 500 dead). Although seemingly mild compared to the levels of violence witnessed elsewhere in Latin America during the period, the Tlatelolco massacre was undeniably traumatic. Mexico had largely been spared the cruel upheavals – military coups, mass killings, urban riots, insurgent movements – that had afflicted other Latin American countries since World War II. Its political system, while far from democratic, was definitely stable. Its economy had grown steadily. It was the envy of the region. But then, in a single, savage blow, Tlatelolco shattered the optimism of many Mexicans who had believed that their country was headed for a bright future of democracy and widely shared prosperity. The regime in power suddenly appeared as a paranoid, obdurate, corrupt, authoritarian monster. "On October 2, 1968, the student movement in Mexico came to an end," wrote Mexican poet Octavio Paz. "So did an entire period of Mexican history."[2]

The president who ordered the massacre, Gustavo Díaz Ordáz, claimed he was proud of his actions, insisting that he had saved Mexico from subversion and catastrophe. His successor, Luis Echeverría, had served as Díaz Ordáz's Secretary of Government, the most powerful cabinet post and a common stepping-stone to the presidency. Echeverría clearly had a hand in the decision to crush the student movement. But unlike Díaz Ordáz, Echeverría seemed almost obsessed with winning over those groups alienated by the government's brutal suppression of the student movement, namely, students, intellectuals, and the middle class in general. This preoccupation led him to preside over an administration that, if arguably not the worst, was certainly the strangest in modern Mexican history.

Upon taking office in 1970, Echeverría announced that he would launch a "democratic opening," and he adopted populist rhetoric, apparently seeking to sell himself as the heir to Lázaro Cárdenas. He enthusiastically championed the import substitution strategy already in place. He denounced the imperialism of the industrialized countries, charging that they used multinational corporations to exploit the labor and resources of the poorer countries. He tried to position Mexico as a leader of the "Third World" movement, pushing a "new economic order" through the United Nations. In 1974 the UN adopted his "Charter of the Economic Rights and Duties of States," which demanded better terms of trade and greater control of resources for developing countries. Echeverría cultivated warm relations with communist Cuba, as well as with Chile's socialist president Salvador Allende. He broke off diplomatic relations with Chile when Allende was overthrown by a violent military coup in 1973.

Closer to home, Echeverría declared amnesty for all those imprisoned as a result of the student demonstrations of 1968, and he undertook a massive increase in government spending, enlarging the bureaucracy from 600,000 employees to over 2 million, which created welcome jobs for graduating students. He tried to win over some of the government's harshest critics by appointing them to exalted positions. Under Echeverría, the budget for the national university grew by nearly 1,700 percent. He imposed some token taxes on businesses and the rich; expanded trade with Europe and Asia; "collectivized" some *ejidos*; carried out an accelerated, though still modest, land redistribution; and worked to establish good relations with Mexicans and Mexican Americans living in the United States. He seemed radical enough to inspire several dozen conservative US Congressmen to send open letters to President Jimmy Carter urging him to do something to prevent Echeverría from leading Mexico to communism.

Most of Echeverría's radicalism was for show. In fact, the Mexican government became, if anything, more corrupt and repressive during the 1970s. In June 1971 government-sponsored goon squads attacked a student demonstration in Mexico City, killing 11 and wounding 200. In both rural and urban areas, Mexico witnessed a level of popular unrest it had not experienced since the 1930s. In the countryside, despite a heralded plan by the World Bank for "investment in the poor," small farmers, who tended rain-fed lands and provided much of the food consumed in Mexico's towns and cities, found that food prices did not keep pace with their costs. Many fled to the cities or to the United States, abandoning nearly 5 million acres of land. By 1980, Mexico – till then, self-sufficient in food production – was forced to import a quarter of the food it consumed. Small-scale growers of corn, already the most marginalized of Mexicans, were hit the hardest by these trends: some 86 percent of them were classified as "underemployed" by the mid-1970s, furnishing an enormous pool of potential migrants.

Some industrial workers bolted the government-controlled unions and formed their own independent unions. Between 1973 and 1977 an estimated 3,600 strikes and labor conflicts were waged, which the government brutally suppressed. In Mexico's poorer states, peasants carried out land invasions, which were likewise met with savage repression. Student and peasant militants formed radical guerrilla organizations, carrying out bombings, bank robberies, kidnappings, and hijackings. By 1975 most of these organizations had been crushed in what is commonly referred to as Mexico's "dirty war." Many dissidents landed in prison, and an untold number simply "disappeared."

Underlying this unrest was Mexico's downward economic spiral that has continued, with lamentably few bright spots, to the present day. Businessmen apparently took Echeverría's populist rhetoric seriously. They retaliated by sending their money abroad and hiking the prices they charged for their products. Meanwhile, foreigners withheld their investments. This, along with the tremendous expansion of the public sector, forced the government to borrow enormous quantities of money from abroad, especially from US banks, increasing the foreign debt sixfold. Rampant inflation cut the average worker's buying power by half. Late in his presidency, Echeverría, at the stern urging of the International Monetary Fund (IMF), was obliged to devalue the peso by about 50 percent.

Even all this bad news was insufficient to persuade the governments of Echeverría and his successor, José López Portillo, to rein in spending. In 1972 new oil fields were found in southeastern Mexico, bumping the nation's proven oil reserves from 10 billion barrels to over 70 billion. Those fields were coming into full exploitation by the end of the 1970s, allowing Mexico to take its place as one of the world's leading petroleum exporters at a time when oil prices were high in the wake of the 1973 Arab oil embargo. Mexican planners were positively drunk with the possibilities this appeared to afford them, spending lavishly and giddily implementing plan after plan aimed at leapfrogging Mexico into the first rank of developed nations. Also during López Portillo's term in office (1976–1982), corruption and abuse of power reached new and appalling heights, leading one insider to lament that corruption, "far from being anecdotal, episodic or exceptional, … tended to become the rule."[3]

Unfortunately for Mexico, the dream of sailing to modernity on a sea of petroleum crashed when oil prices plummeted in the early 1980s, leaving Mexico with a foreign debt of $85 billion which, with an economic growth rate of zero, it had little hope of repaying. Adding to the nation's misery, world interest rates rose and commercial banks reduced their lending. López Portillo reluctantly devalued the peso in February 1982, and soon Mexico's currency was in free fall. In August, Mexico announced that it was forced to suspend debt payments for 90 days, and the following month López Portillo, scapegoating bankers for the crisis, without warning nationalized every private bank in the country. Hyperinflation, capital flight, and general economic chaos prevailed in Mexico for the remainder of the decade. Runaway inflation caused Mexicans' buying power to fall by an average of 5 percent per year between 1983 and 1988. As if economic chaos were not enough, nature did its bit to increase the misery with a severe earthquake in 1985 that killed nearly 10,000 people and devastated much of downtown Mexico City. The Mexican government's inept and cynical response to the tragedy only added to the trauma. Mexico's "miracle" was a faded memory.

The 1980s was a period of tremendous hardship and dramatic change. Mexico became a "model debtor" country, obediently following the prescriptions of international lenders at a time when the loudest voices in governments and universities argued for a full-bore revival of classical economic ideas. The key to economic success, according to this line of thinking, was to expand the private sector, shrink the public sector, deregulate, cut taxes and tariffs and subsidies, and generally allow the invisible hand of the marketplace to set the economic agenda.

The 1980s is sometimes called Mexico's "lost decade," though that phrase does little justice to the reality many Mexicans endured. In 1982 a large portion of Mexico's population already lived in deplorable conditions, with nearly 20 million people suffering malnutrition, illiteracy, inadequate healthcare, and lack of the most basic amenities of modern life such as running water and electricity. But things could, people soon learned, get much worse. The government was obliged to devote such a large part of its revenues to debt servicing that there was little left for "social spending," which had been woefully inadequate even during the fabled boom times. Spending on education and health – already scandalously low – contracted by 33 percent, and subsidies were eliminated on corn, beans, cooking oil, bread, and eggs. Deaths from malnutrition increased, more kids dropped out of school, and property crimes skyrocketed. The rich were able to shelter their fortunes from negative trends by simply stashing their funds in foreign bank accounts: it is estimated that somewhere between $22 billion and $36 billion in much-needed capital fled Mexico between 1977 and 1987. The poor and middle class, of course, did not have the luxury of squirreling their money away in foreign banks, and so they got poorer as the rich held fast, further exacerbating inequality in what was already one of the world's most unequal societies. One economist ran a few figures and came to a startling conclusion: if Mexico were to continue with the rate of economic growth that prevailed in the late 1980s, it would take the poorest 10 percent of Mexicans nearly 50 years to work their way up to a level of "extreme poverty" (about $200 a year).[4]

Not surprisingly, during the 1980s emigrating illegally to the United States proved a popular option. The "safety valve" function of that emigration was most likely an important factor in ensuring that the deplorable conditions in Mexico did not lead to widespread civil and political unrest. During the 1980s and early 1990s the number of "alien apprehensions" in the United States – an imperfect but inevitable measure of the numbers of border crossers – averaged 1,260,855 a year, a 50 percent increase from the 1970s.

After the Bracero Program

In 1955 the INS had boasted that, due to its heroic efforts in "Operation Wetback," the "wetback problem no longer exists." The gathering crisis in Mexico made a mockery of that boast. There was a lull in illegal migration between 1954 and 1965, but 1964–1965 saw the end of the Bracero Program and an ambitious rewriting of immigration law, which together breathed new life into the illegal flows, till by the mid-1970s Americans were once again decrying a "crisis" over illegal immigration.

The two key events – the end of the Bracero Program and the new immigration law – actually had similar origins, namely, the growing sway of liberals in US politics. Senators like Hubert Humphrey, John F. Kennedy, and Herbert Lehman believed that immigration was closely linked to civil rights. Just as they believed the Bracero Program exploited Mexicans while worsening conditions for American workers, they believed that the prevailing immigration law was racist, for it gave preference to white European immigrants on the grounds that they were more assimilable with the majority of Americans. Although the exclusion of

Asians had been ended immediately after World War II, visas were still awarded according to the "national origins" formula that had been devised in 1924. Liberals believed that the "national origins" criteria were incompatible with the notion that the United States was a generous country, happy to welcome all peoples to its shores regardless of race, ethnicity, or nationality. The Cold War was a necessary backdrop to the liberals' concerns, for they were at pains to demonstrate that the United States was a land of freedom and equality, in clear contrast to its communist antagonists. As a group of Democratic Congressmen wrote, "It is intolerable that we should continue to maintain our own Iron Curtain – against visitors and alien immigrants alike – while criticizing the Iron Curtain abroad."[5] Unlike the architects of the 1924 "national origins" immigration plan, who were keen to keep the country ethnically homogeneous, the new generation of liberals saw strength in diversity. One such thinker argued that the metaphor of the American melting pot was all wrong. "The true image of America," he said, "is the kaleidoscope. It is a mosaic of human beings that is always changing but encased in a basic framework of freedom, of brotherhood, of tolerance, of creativity."[6]

Along with the waxing influence of reformist liberals was a fairly stunning shift in the views of organized labor, long one of the loudest voices in favor of immigration restriction. The American Federation of Labor (AFL) merged with the more liberal-minded Congress of Industrial Organizations (CIO) in 1955. The CIO's membership included a large number of first- and second-generation immigrants, many of whom had been targets of earlier restrictionist campaigns. George Meany, the AFL-CIO's first president, believed that the national origins system was racist and discriminatory. He quickly purged the organization of leaders who had championed immigration restriction. From that point onward, organized labor became a leading advocate for a generous and expansive immigration policy.

Oddly, the debate surrounding the immigration reform of 1965 omitted discussion of the Western Hemisphere generally, and of undocumented Mexican immigrants specifically, as if those were entirely separate matters, unrelated to mainstream immigration. Most of the peoples of the Western Hemisphere had been exempt from the restrictionist quotas of 1924, although the McCarran-Walter Act of 1952 did impose quotas on immigration from the former British colonies in the Caribbean in order to limit the numbers of black immigrants. Like their more conservative counterparts, the liberal reformers tended to see legitimate immigration emanating from Europe and Asia, while Mexican immigration, in the words of one reformer, "swarms in at the back door and through the windows."[7] Liberal reformers were certainly guilty of their own form of racism.

The Immigration Act of 1965 – also known as the Hart-Cellar Act – officially abolished the national origins quotas, substituting a worldwide limit of 290,000 immigrants per year, with a 20,000-person limit per country. In place of race or nationality, preference was given to professionals and people with desirable skills, and for family reunification. The Eastern Hemisphere – that is, Europe, Asia, and Africa – was awarded 170,000 slots. The Western Hemisphere became subject to quotas for the first time, its limit placed at 120,000, without per-country limits or preferences. In a nod toward organized labor, the Department of Labor was enjoined to certify that there were not enough domestic workers to do the jobs sought by Western Hemisphere immigrants, and that employment of such immigrants would not lower wages or worsen working conditions. The reform was billed as a major correction to historic injustices. President Lyndon B. Johnson introduced the Act with stirring rhetoric. "Every American," he said, "can be proud today because we have finally eliminated the cruel and unjust national origins system from the immigration policy of the United States. We have righted a longstanding wrong. So today, any man, anywhere in the world can hope to begin a new life of freedom and a new life of greater opportunity in the United States. No longer will his color or his religion or his nationality be a barrier to him."[8]

In 1976 Congress amended the Act to impose a quota of 20,000 on individual countries of the Americas, at the same time closing a loophole in the law that had allowed Mexicans who gave birth to children in the United States to become legal residents. Eager not to discriminate among the countries of the hemisphere, the amended law ignored the element of demand in determining the supply of visas, making no exception for the two countries that traditionally sent the most migrants to the United States, namely its neighbors, Canada and Mexico. Thus, despite a series of proposals to raise the quota for "contiguous countries," Mexico in the end was allotted precisely the same number of visas as Uruguay, even though Uruguay is 5,000 miles from the United States and has about a thirtieth the number of people. By drastically restricting the possibility of legal immigration from Mexico at a time when more and more Mexicans were desperate to find work in the United States, the 1965 law and its 1976 amendment guaranteed that the bulk of Mexican immigrants would be "illegal."

Not surprisingly, the numbers of "illegal aliens" skyrocketed after the new law went into effect in 1968. In that year, 151,000 undocumented Mexicans were deported; in 1976, when the 20,000 per country quota went into effect, the number rose to 781,000 – nearly eight times the total number of undocumented immigrants from the rest of the countries in the world combined. In a development that seems to have taken the immigration reformers by surprise, the numbers of Mexicans legally admitted to the United States also continued to rise precipitously, since the emphasis on family reunification meant that each immigrant was permitted to bring in family members above the quota limit. Even so, the Immigration Act of 1965 and its 1976 amendment had the effect of making the term "illegal alien" practically synonymous with "Mexican." Worse, since the reform had been sold as "fair" and non-discriminatory, favoring no country over any other, undocumented Mexican immigrants were stigmatized as criminals who could only be controlled through law enforcement measures, a fact that likely contributed to the growing popular panic over the perceived "alien invasion" of the 1970s and 1980s.

Making matters worse was the global economic recession of the mid-1970s. Just as in the Great Depression, economic hardship tended to focus people's attention on the presence of illegal immigrants. Wayne Cornelius, a longtime leading immigration scholar, put it this way: "Something quite predictable happens in the United States every time the economy goes through difficult times: illegal workers are rediscovered. Politicians, journalists, organized labor, and other pressure groups run to blame them for all the possible or imaginary problems that may exist in American society."[9]

Other developments in the 1970s and 1980s tended to provoke nativist reactions in the United States. The 1965 Immigration Act profoundly changed the character of immigration to the United States, so that non-white, "Third World" peoples came to comprise the bulk of immigrants.

And in several instances, non-white people arrived in ways that attracted special attention. America's loss of the Vietnam War was followed by the arrival of a wave of some 130,000 Asian "boat people" on American shores. In October 1980 some 125,000 refugees were allowed to leave Cuba for Florida in what became known as the Mariel Boatlift. Cuban dictator Fidel Castro, hoping to damage the image of Cuban refugees, made sure that a large number of delinquents were among the refugees, which helped to further cement the linkage between Latinos, immigration, and criminality in the minds of many Americans. With the advanced mechanization of agriculture, Mexican workers increasingly found employment in areas such as hotels, restaurants, domestic service, construction, and light industry, which made them more visible to American city dwellers. The 1960s and 1970s also witnessed the rise of activism among Mexican Americans, with some of the more radical Chicano groups floating the notion of creating a "Republic of Aztlán" out of the lands that the United States had taken from Mexico in 1848. Some Americans feared that the Southwest was destined to become an "American Quebec" – that is, an ethnically and linguistically distinct region that would weaken the unity of the nation-state. The tone of the rhetoric surrounding the issue of illegal immigration turned ugly rather quickly.

Ex-Marine General Leonard Chapman, Immigration and Naturalization Service chief under Presidents Nixon and Ford, helped to set the tone by explicitly blaming US economic woes on illegal immigrants and wildly exaggerating their numbers. Ford's Attorney General William Saxby chimed in to call illegal immigration a "severe national crisis" that was causing unemployment, increased crime, and higher welfare costs. President Ford himself opined in 1976 that "the main problem is how to get rid of those 6 to 8 million aliens who are interfering with our economic prosperity." CIA chief William Colby outdid them all in the production of overheated rhetoric. "The most obvious threat [for the United States]," said Colby, "is the fact that there are 60 million Mexicans today and there are going to be 120 million Mexicans by the end of the century … [The Border Patrol] will not have enough bullets to stop them."[10]

Other groups suggested different reasons for opposing illegal immigration. Liberals like Minnesota Democrat Walter Mondale feared that illegal immigration might harm organized labor and derail anti-poverty campaigns. In 1968 National Farm Workers' Association leader César Chávez sought help from Congressional allies when illegal immigrants were brought in to break the grape pickers' strike he had organized. Liberals also worried that illegal immigrants comprised a vulnerable subclass of people – a "shadow population," in the words of Supreme Court Justice William Brennan – who worked for a pittance but had no political rights, no legal protections, and no reliable access to basic services such as medical care and education for their children.

Oddly, given this atmosphere of crisis, the initiative to do something about illegal immigration, which began in Congress in the early 1970s, took nearly a decade and a half to result in actual legislation. Moreover, by the time that legislation passed it had been tweaked by such varied and vociferous interest groups that it had little hope of actually achieving its stated purpose.

The opening salvo for reform came in 1971, when New Jersey Democrat Peter Rodino, chair of the House Judiciary Committee's Subcommittee on Immigration, began hearings on illegal immigration. Rodino's subcommittee heard from local politicians, ethnic advocacy and civil rights groups, labor organizers, religious organizations, and others. These groups were unanimous in their contention that illegal immigrants cost American jobs and worsened working conditions. They were also unanimous in their recommendation that the best way to fix the problem was to impose sanctions on the employers of illegal workers – sanctions with real teeth, so that illegal immigrants would be unable to find work in the United States. The idea was hardly new. The Mexican government had been pleading for just such a measure for years. Senator Paul Douglas of Illinois had proposed it as an amendment to the McCarran-Walter Immigration Act back in 1952, but it had been soundly defeated by a group of powerful Texas senators with strong ties to big agriculture.

Rodino introduced his first employer sanctions bill in 1972. The bill sailed through the House, but ran into trouble in the Senate. There, Senator James Eastland, who had controlled the Judiciary Committee since 1956, had no intention of considering even the mildest of employer sanctions. A Mississippi Democrat best remembered for his virulent white supremacist views, Eastland had close ties to big growers who benefited from cheap, illegal Mexican labor. Despite the undoubted popularity of doing something to control illegal immigration, Eastland refused to allow the Senate Judiciary Committee to take any action on Rodino's measure. When Rodino reintroduced his bill in 1973, it once again was overwhelmingly approved in the House, but met the same fate in the Senate.

Since Eastland controlled top appointments to the Immigration and Naturalization Service, it is not surprising that during the 1960s and early 1970s the INS was practically flaunting its lack of concern about the illegal immigration issue. Top INS officials appeared before Congress each year to request only minimal appropriations for their agency and for the Border Patrol, insisting that the problem of illegal immigration had been greatly overblown. It was only when complaints about the steadily growing volume of illegal immigration became impossible to ignore that President Richard Nixon replaced Eastland's man with retired Marine Corps General Leonard Chapman, a man whose views on illegal immigration were positively alarmist.

The tide was moving against old guard stalwarts like Eastland, but the passage of a meaningful employer sanctions bill still faced daunting obstacles. Ethnic rights groups and some unions feared that employer sanctions would give employers cover if they decided to discriminate against job applicants merely because they looked or sounded "foreign." Among these groups were the Mexican-American Legal Defense and Education Fund (MALDEF) and the National Council of La Raza (NCLR), both Hispanic advocacy groups formed in the late 1960s and early 1970s. César Chávez changed his tune on illegal immigration in the early 1970s, saying he opposed only those illegal immigrants who served as strikebreakers. The International Ladies' Garment Workers Union, denouncing government inaction on illegal immigration, declared that it intended to begin organizing illegal immigrants working in the garment industry. Such groups joined forces with a variety of grower and big business groups, who claimed that employer sanctions not only threatened to deprive them of needed workers, but such sanctions would be overly costly and impossible to enforce. Ethnic advocacy groups and big business were odd bedfellows, having very different reasons for opposing employer sanctions. But, as one MALDEF leader put it in 1982, "I would dance with the devil if I had to" to defeat the measure.[11]

Lining up in favor of employer sanctions were the usual suspects – nativists, organized labor, liberal politicians, and some ethnic advocacy groups that maintained job displacement was a more salient issue than possible discrimination – plus a few newcomers to the fight. Biologist Paul Ehrlich's 1968 bestseller, *The Population Bomb*, focused attention on the problem of overpopulation and the role of immigration in adding to that problem in the developed countries. Environmentalists also entered the fray, claiming that immigrants not only added to the strain on resources, but they often hailed from cultures that had scant reverence for the environment. In 1979 Michigan ophthalmologist and environmentalist John Tanton, together with environmental lawyer Roger Conner, founded the Federation for American Immigration Reform (FAIR) to push for restrictionist policies.

In 1977 President Jimmy Carter issued his own comprehensive plan to control illegal immigration. The plan included harsh employer sanctions, the use of social security cards to verify employment eligibility, enhanced interdiction at the US–Mexico border, and amnesty for illegal immigrants who had been in the United States since before 1970. Although this was the basic formula for virtually all existing immigration reform bill proposals, Carter's failure to consult with Congress and the intense mobilization of opposition groups stopped Carter's proposals in their tracks.

In the wake of this defeat, Carter, at the urging of Massachusetts Senator Edward Kennedy, took the important step of appointing a commission to study immigration and to make recommendations on reform. The Select Commission on Immigration and Refugee Policy (SCIRP) began its work in 1978 under the leadership of Theodore Hesburgh, a Catholic priest, president of Notre Dame University, and a former head of the Civil Rights Commission. The committee also included cabinet secretaries, Congress members, and several private citizens. The Congressional contingent included Senators Alan Simpson (R-WY) and Edward Kennedy (D-MA), who would soon join forces to usher several bills through Congress.

SCIRP issued its findings in 1981, in a report entitled *US Immigration and the National Interest*. The report was exuberant in its praise for legal immigration, arguing for a generous immigration policy that did not discriminate on the basis of race, ethnicity, nationality, or religion. On the other hand, the report excoriated illegal immigration on a number of grounds. Illegal immigration created a population of vulnerable people with no rights or protections, undercutting the "principle that all who live and work in the US, regardless of ethnicity, should have fundamental rights."[12] Tolerating illegal immigration, the report argued, bred disrespect for the rule of law, especially immigration law. As for specific policy recommendations, SCIRP's proposals did not differ greatly from Carter's: SCIRP endorsed employer sanctions, advocated beefing up the Border Patrol, and suggested a generous amnesty program for illegal immigrants already in the United States. In a controversial wrinkle, SCIRP recommended the use of a national identification card as the basis for employment eligibility – a suggestion that was quickly denounced by liberal politicians and civil rights groups as a violation of privacy and creeping totalitarianism. The SCIRP report also came out in opposition to a new large-scale guest worker scheme along the lines of the defunct Bracero Program, insisting it would lead to greater exploitation. The essential observations of SCIRP – that legal immigration was a positive force that should be encouraged and that illegal immigration was a menace that should be curtailed – proved enormously influential during the 1980s, such that most of the reform bills that were introduced during that period were at pains to justify their provisions with a respectful nod in SCIRP's direction.

The first legislative proposal to appear in the wake of SCIRP's report was drafted by Alan Simpson and Kentucky Congressman Romano Mazzoli and introduced in early 1982. Although by that time close to 1,000 illegal entrants were being deported each day, and polls showed overwhelming support for anti-illegal immigration measures, the bill was greeted by ferocious lobbying on the part of employer and ethnic groups and never made it out of the House. Congressional Democrats were reluctant to advance such a bill, since two of their key constituencies – organized labor and ethnic lobbies – were at odds about employer sanctions. House Speaker Thomas P. "Tip" O'Neill was concerned about the political calculus of the bill, fearing if it passed, President Ronald Reagan might veto it in order to curry favor with Hispanics.

Reagan, for his part, was conflicted. At heart a free market fundamentalist, he saw little problem with opening the border. During his 1980 presidential campaign, Reagan spoke of creating a free trade zone that would encompass all of North America, in which goods, services, technology, and people would all move freely. Reagan also had strong ties to southwestern agribusiness interests, which believed the border should be open to all comers. Furthermore, Reagan had no use for government regulation of the economy, and he warned against the red tape that would surely creep into any effective employer sanctions program. On the other hand, some members of the Reagan administration were very alarmed indeed about illegal immigration. In this camp was Attorney General William French Smith, who famously warned that "we have lost control of our borders" – a remark that is often echoed, yet fundamentally odd, for it assumes, incorrectly, that at some point the United States actually *had* control of its borders.

In general, the Republican position during the 1980s and 1990s favored doing little that might actually impede illegal immigration, while denying illegal – and even legal – immigrants access to civil rights and political protection. The growing free-for-all at the border, where massive numbers of people entered at the same time as massive numbers of people were expelled, ensured that illegal immigrants would work hard and keep a low profile, never engaging in any activity that might actually improve their status.

With so many conflicting interests in the fight, there were relatively few politicians who saw any real advantage in pushing the immigration issue. Over and over, immigration reform bills died, only to be revived again and again. Senator Alan Simpson deserves much of the credit for ensuring the reform bill's multiple resurrections. Simpson had been a member of the SCIRP committee, and he became a prominent apologist for its views. The formula he championed through numerous setbacks was by now entirely familiar: employer sanctions (which he referred to as "the guts of controlling illegal immigration"); better border enforcement; and legalization for some who were in the United States illegally. Simpson also recommended that a "more secure worker verification system" be devised, though on this point he was somewhat vague. His bill envisioned the use of "existing" documents such as passports, birth certificates, driver's licenses, Social Security cards, or alien registration cards. Foreseeing the possibility that such documents could be forged, the bill called for a review after three years to determine if something more "secure" was needed, but the legislation ruled out the use of "national ID cards." The bill also barred newly legalized aliens from receiving federal public assistance benefits for a period of three to six years.

In a 1984 article in defense of his bill, Simpson reviewed – and made short work of – several "counter proposals." He rejected a new temporary guest worker program not because it would be exploitative, but because he claimed that temporary workers often "become permanent," they create foreign policy problems, and they "tend to stimulate illegal immigration." As evidence for the last point he noted that the Bracero Program was accompanied by a steep rise in illegal immigration, but failed to note that the practice of "drying out" – something analogous to the "amnesty" program contained in his own bill – was a major factor in encouraging workers to enter the country illegally. Simpson also dismissed more restrictionist approaches on the grounds that they would "dilute our traditionally generous policies of legal immigration and refugee admissions," and that, without an amnesty provision, they "would not address the problem of an illegal immigrant subclass in the US."

Simpson was also less than sanguine about an idea that had been floated for years by, among others, the Reverend Paul Empie of the National Lutheran Council. Such critics of US immigration policy were dismayed that the immigration problem was nearly always treated unilaterally by the United States, usually as an issue of enforcement. Empie thought that the United States should use "our resources in such a way as to help such persons in countries where they are."[13] Simpson contended that Mexico's economy was in crisis, that merely to break even it would have to create a daunting 750,000 new jobs each year, and that in the short term rising incomes might stimulate rather than halt migration (presumably, though Simpson did not explain this point, because very poor people have a harder time absorbing the costs and risks of international migration). Although nearly all proposals for dealing with illegal immigration made some token mention of uplifting the economies of poor countries, they routinely came around to the same conclusion as Simpson, that "such initiatives are no substitute for domestic immigration reform." Simpson minimized the difficulties that enforcing employer sanctions and closing off the border to illegal entrants would entail – tasks that would arguably be as daunting and as costly as improving Mexico's economy. Nor did he raise the possibility of revising the structure of US–Mexican economic relations in ways that might bring greater benefits to Mexico.[14]

The short shrift that Simpson and other immigration reformers gave to the notion of including Mexico in discussions of immigration reform raises the question of precisely what role Mexico *did* play in these initiatives. The short answer is, virtually none – the United States acted altogether unilaterally in determining immigration policy. Since at least the 1910s, Mexican officials had striven for a voice in setting US immigration policies. They had seen large-scale emigration to the United States as a national embarrassment, something they wished actively to combat. They were especially distressed by illegal migration, occasionally taking steps to curtail it and repeatedly assailing the United States for its inaction on the matter. But by the mid-1970s Mexico had virtually withdrawn from the discussion, a dramatic departure from its earlier posture.

There were several reasons for Mexico's new apparent indifference toward the migration issue, and its tendency not to interject itself into US policy debates. For one, Mexico, having had its territory invaded on many occasions, was a great defender of the principle of non-intervention in the affairs of other, sovereign nations. Mexican leaders were likely also aware that any meddling would be met with such hostility that it could prove counterproductive. As if to prove the point, Colorado Governor Richard Lamm belligerently warned Mexico that it had no right to "a determining voice in our policy-making process."[15]

Also, in the heady days of the mid-1970s, Mexican officials were excited by the possibility of rapid, petroleum-fueled economic development, and they were especially suspicious that any apparent concessions on the part of the United States might actually be cynical bargaining tactics aimed at taking advantage of Mexico's good fortune. Although Mexican officials had opposed the termination of the Bracero Program during the early 1960s, and spent the next decade pleading for its reinstatement, in 1974 they showed no enthusiasm when President Gerald Ford and his Secretary of State Henry Kissinger, their appetite piqued by new oil discoveries in Mexico, allowed that "some thought has been given to the possibility of negotiating a new agreement."[16] As early as 1972, President Luis Echeverría had declared that the solution to the emigration problem was economic and social development within Mexico. He told US officials that "we want to export merchandise, not social problems."[17]

According to scholar and diplomat Carlos Rico, Mexican officials drastically reassessed the entire issue of migration during the 1970s. The traditional reasons Mexico had sanctioned emigration were to export part of Mexico's unemployment problem, reap the economic benefits of emigrants' remittances, and keep open a "safety valve" to decrease social tensions and siphon off potential troublemakers. The rationale for urging a renewal of the Bracero Program had entailed all of these factors, plus the sense that a formal agreement was the best guarantee that the rights of Mexican workers in the United States would be respected. But by the 1970s there had been ample time to assess the Bracero Program, and Mexicans recognized that such agreements did not necessarily ensure protection of workers' rights: the abuses within the Bracero Program, particularly in its later stages, had been infamous. Illegal migrants probably would not fare all that much worse.

Mexican officials had also decided that, with regard to migration, the status quo was preferable to most of the other possible scenarios. The migration between Mexico and the United States was, for the most part, circular. Most emigrants went to the United States to work, with no intention of remaining there. The temporary nature of their sojourns, plus the racial discrimination they sometimes faced in the United States, gave them little reason to try to blend in, learn English, and adopt American customs. This likely harmed the migrants' interests in the long run, for it led many Americans to suppose that Mexicans were "unassimilable," when in fact studies have shown that, for those who are determined to put down roots, integration patterns of Mexican immigrants and their offspring are identical to those of other immigrant groups. For Mexican officials, however, temporary migration was a desirable phenomenon. Emigrants were among the most enterprising members of their communities, so the long-run impact of permanent migration would be to deprive Mexico of much talent. Returnees, on the other hand, would presumably bring whatever skills they had acquired while abroad and, perhaps, use those skills for Mexico's benefit.

Beyond that, Mexican officials made some basic assumptions. They came to see the migration question as a relatively simple matter of supply and demand: many sectors of the US economy needed low-cost labor so badly that, should they be deprived of such labor, some businesses would go under, others would mechanize their operations, and still others would send their operations offshore. Mexican immigrants did not displace US workers, Mexican officials came to believe, because they only took jobs American citizens were unwilling to do. Finally, and perhaps most crucially, Mexican officials reasoned that Mexican migration responded to powerful economic laws, and was relatively impervious to government control. That is to say, Mexicans figured that the discussions going on in US official circles were an exercise in futility, for none of the measures the United States might adopt held much prospect of stanching the flow of migrants in any case. The Mexicans would have preferred that the United States and Mexico pursue a bilateral approach to *regulating* a flow of humanity that could not, ultimately, be stopped. But they seldom made an issue of this preference, since they recognized that their own assumptions were so far removed from those that prevailed in US debates that there was little chance of productive dialogue.

On the US side, there were a few meager attempts to involve Mexico in the discussions. The most ambitious such effort was undertaken by President Jimmy Carter after the failure of the immigration plan he proposed in 1977. Carter ordered the National Security Council to undertake a review of US–Mexican relations. A committee was formed involving all branches of the executive department, and a new office of "Mexican Affairs Coordinator" was set up in the State Department. The plan was to have the committee and its working groups identify priorities and possible trade-offs that might ease tensions and smooth policy-making in the future. Unfortunately, this initiative did little beyond identifying a few areas of concern. Soon, President Carter's attention was distracted by such developments as the Soviet invasion of Afghanistan, the Sandinista revolution in Nicaragua and deteriorating situation in Central America, and the Iranian hostage crisis. US–Mexican relations receded into the background.[18]

Opening Wide the Gates: The Immigration Reforms of 1986 and 1990

With Mexico grudgingly resolved to let the United States proceed unilaterally on immigration matters, American policy-makers needed to heed only those voices that made themselves heard on the domestic front.

Such voices were not in short supply. Although the decade of the 1980s began with many shrill pronouncements about out-of-control borders and calls for restriction, it ended with some of the most generous invitations to increased migration since the nineteenth century. Writing in 1979, Paul Ehrlich, a prominent population control advocate and FAIR member, was able accurately to predict the outcome of the contest. "In immigration legislation, the restrictionists are usually strong enough to get the law written their way, but the anti-restrictionists, particularly the employers, are strong enough to write the loopholes."[19]

At the start of the 1980s, popular sentiment seems squarely to have been in favor of curtailing immigration. The alarm caused by the massive influx of Indochinese, Cuban, and Haitian refugees in the early 1980s, the recession of 1980–1982, and a general reticence of policy-makers to tackle immigration matters, which was widely seen as a lose-lose political issue, all suggested that the direction of immigration reform would continue, as it had since roughly 1910, in the direction of restricting the flow.

But several potent factors ultimately capsized efforts to restrict immigration. In the first years of the decade the judicial branch began to involve itself in immigration matters for the first time in US history. The Supreme Court determined that the Reagan administration, as well as some state and local governments, were acting arbitrarily and overzealously in their efforts to limit the rights of refugees and immigrants, and it issued a number of rulings aimed at correcting those abuses. The landmark ruling came in 1982 in the case of *Plyler v. Doe* (457 US 202), which said that states could not deny public education to the children of undocumented immigrants. Writing for the majority, Justice William Brennan noted that the equal protection clause of the Fourteenth Amendment "extends to anyone, citizen or stranger, who is subject to the laws of the state." Brennan's ruling pointedly criticized people who benefited from the labor of undocumented immigrants but who nonetheless sought to deny those immigrants basic rights. "This situation," Brennan wrote, "raises the specter of a permanent caste of undocumented resident aliens, encouraged by some to remain here as a source of cheap labor, but nevertheless denied the benefits our society makes available to citizens and lawful residents."[20] Other court rulings made it easier for immigrants to resist deportation and made it harder for the government to exclude controversial persons from the United States on ideological grounds.

The civil rights movement had tended to move public opinion in the direction of greater acceptance of diversity, such that xenophobic and racist language played virtually no part in the debates of the 1980s (that kind of language would be revived in subsequent decades). By that time, many strange bedfellows – ethnic groups, human rights defenders, big business, many academics and politicians enthralled with the new vogue of free market fundamentalism – were in perfect agreement that legal immigration was a good thing. Adding their voices to the pro-immigration chorus were certain politicians who had come to believe that the United States was in danger of falling behind in the increasingly globalized economy. These politicians reckoned that at least part of the problem was a shortage of people with the right kinds of skills to make the United States more competitive. Attracting the "right kind" of immigrants, then, was crucial to America's future, and doing so would entail changing some of the rules of legal immigration. But at the same time, most reformers agreed that, before new and more generous reforms could be enacted, the "back door" would have to be sealed, that is, illegal immigration would have to be controlled, or at least appear to be controlled.

In the final horse-trading that preceded the passage of the Immigration Reform and Control Act (IRCA) of 1986, Congress made significant concessions to powerful interest groups. State and local governments were mollified by federal subsidies, while liberals, ethnic organizations, and human rights advocates were reassured by stringent anti-discrimination and worker protection provisions, as well as by a remarkably generous amnesty program for illegal immigrants. The big winners in the IRCA legislation – as in so many past reforms – were business and employer interests. When it seemed likely that the bill had little chance of passage, Democratic Congressman Chuck Schumer of New York hammered out a deal that gave major concessions to the growers of perishable crops. In addition to a large agricultural guest worker program (referred to as "H-2A"), a legalization program was implemented specifically for agricultural workers; if those newly legal-ized workers should seek greener pastures elsewhere, there were to be provisions to replenish the agricultural labor supply as needed.

The Texas Proviso was finally abolished, and employment of an illegal immigrant was formally outlawed, with stiff penalties prescribed for violators. But, at the employers' insistence, this provision was made toothless by a massive loophole and by the absence of any sort of secure identification system. While employers were forbidden to "knowingly" hire undocumented workers, IRCA supplied them with a ready-made defense in case they did so. Employers had to fill out an Employment Eligibility Verification Form (I-9) stating that they had examined the documents proffered by a prospective employee, but they had no obligation to check the authenticity of those documents. So long as they maintained that they had "complied in good faith" with the law's requirements, they were entirely off the hook. The chief effect of the legislation was to create a flourishing trade in bogus documents.

Undoubtedly IRCA's most enduring legacy was its amnesty program. The legislation allowed undocumented immigrants who could prove that they had resided in the United States continuously since January 1, 1982 to apply for adjustment of status. Applicants for legalization were to apply within 18 months from the time the law went into effect; after a year in the transitional status of "lawful temporary resident," applicants would be required to demonstrate a minimal command of English and US history and government, provisions that in the past had only been demanded of applicants for full citizenship. Applicants were also liable for application fees as well as charges for medical inspection, photographs, fingerprints, and sometimes legal counsel, all of which typically amounted to more than $1,000 for a family of four. Despite the difficulties and expense, roughly 3 million undocumented immigrants were legalized after 1986, including 1.3 million "special agricultural workers" or SAWs, and 1.7 million "legally authorized workers" or LAWs. The standards implemented to prove such residence were so relaxed, and fraud was so widespread, that, according to one estimate, the number of people legalized under the SAW program in California was three times the total number of farm workers in the state at the time.

It soon became apparent that IRCA was not working as it had been intended. In fact, although there was a decline in border apprehensions for the first three years after its enactment, after 1989 illegal crossings rose once again. Despite ample evidence to the contrary, Congress was apparently satisfied that IRCA had successfully closed the "back door" – that is, put an end to illegal immigration – so it now focused its attention on reforming *legal* immigration, in the form of the Immigration Act of 1990. Some analysts went so far as to conclude that IRCA had been largely symbolic, "a political 'cover' for liberalizing our immigration laws."[21]

The 1990 immigration reform expanded immigration to the United States. It raised the ceiling on immigration worldwide from 290,000 to 700,000 during a three-year "transition period," after which the ceiling was reduced to 675,000. It also imposed caps on different categories of immigrants, with 480,000 visas set aside for family reunification, 140,000 for persons who possessed desirable skills, and 55,000 for "diversity." Ironically, by "diversity" the framers of the Act had in mind nationalities that had been "adversely affected" by the 1965 immigration reform, so most of those visas went to people from Ireland, Great Britain, Canada, and Poland – nationalities that were already well represented within the American population. The per-country cap was raised from 20,000 to 25,620. The family based category was whittled down in a complex formula whereby immediate relatives of US citizens could enter the country free from numerical restrictions, but the number of such entrants would be subtracted from the following year's quota of 480,000 family based immigrants. With this provision, Congress hoped to cut down the numbers of siblings and other more distant relatives entering, and to give preference to spouses and more immediate relations. The 1990 Act also provided funding to add another 1,000 Border Patrol agents, made employer sanctions a bit stricter, increased penalties for many immigration violations, and streamlined deportation procedures for criminals.

There was some discussion – as there had been since the imposition of numerical quotas on Western Hemisphere countries in 1976 – of increasing the number of visas available to "contiguous countries," namely Mexico and Canada, but the point was dropped. Still, Mexico benefited from the fact that three quarters of the spouses and young children (under 21) of legal permanent residents were exempted from the per-country limits. Mexico remained the leading source of both legal and illegal immigrants under the new legislation, while in global terms, the 1990 Act increased all immigration significantly.

The immigration reforms of 1986 and 1990 altered the American public's perception of Mexican immigration. One of the problems bequeathed by the Reagan and George H. W. Bush administrations was their tendency to conflate the several problems that the border had come to represent. The border was the place where illegal immigrants crossed into the United States; it was a place where massive and increasing quantities of illicit drugs entered the country; and it was also the vulnerable frontier of a nation that appeared to be growing ever more insecure. Reagan himself, in attempting to justify his interventions in the conflicts in Central America, conjured the specter of communist throngs penetrating the United States through Harlingen, Texas. The end result of that conflation was that, in the minds of many Americans, undocumented Mexican workers came to represent a threat similar to those alien contagions – enervating drugs and subversive ideologies – the sort of toxins that might sap the national spirit. All of this ensured that, unlike the relatively genteel conversations of the 1980s, the rhetoric that infected the debates of the 1990s and early 2000s reached a level of hostility not seen since the 1920s.

5

Free Trade and Homeland Security

1990–Present

The enthusiasm for "neoliberalism" – privatization, deregulation, free trade, and shrinking the public sector – that prevailed in Washington during the 1980s led to the signing of a North American Free Trade Agreement (NAFTA) in 1994. The agreement obliged its three signatories (the US, Canada, and Mexico) to carry out internal reforms and to eliminate tariffs and other impediments to free trade. The proponents of NAFTA declared that the agreement would lift Mexico out of poverty, putting a definitive end to the immigration problem.

The results were disappointing to say the least. Upon the signing of NAFTA – though not necessarily because of NAFTA – Mexico entered into a period of turmoil, propelling more of its citizens than ever to head north to participate in the relatively robust US economy. The sudden and dramatic increase in cross-border trade and traffic between Mexico and the United States brought on by NAFTA was accompanied by a vehement nativist reaction in the United States that demanded an effective closing of the borders – two trends that pushed in exactly opposite directions. The anxieties of US citizens regarding Mexican immigration were intensified by the increasing geographic dispersal of Mexican immigrants away from their traditional destinations in the Southwest and Chicago, as well as by the terrorist attacks of September 11, 2001, which caused national security to shoot to the top of the list of American

Beyond Borders: A History of Mexican Migration to the United States
By Timothy J. Henderson
© 2011 Timothy J. Henderson

concerns. Taken all together, developments after 1994 made for one of the most volatile periods in the history of Mexican immigration to the United States.

The North American Free Trade Agreement

By the late 1980s the turmoil in Mexico's economy had begun to abate somewhat. In 1989 the ruling party candidate, Carlos Salinas de Gortari, ran against Cuauhtémoc Cárdenas, son of 1930s president Lázaro Cárdenas and the candidate of a coalition of leftist parties that was dubbed the Party of the Democratic Revolution (PRD). The election was marred by serious "irregularities," and Salinas de Gortari assumed the office of president amid a cloud of ill will and skepticism.

In many ways, Salinas was cut from a different mold from previous Mexican presidents. He held two master's degrees and a Harvard doctorate in government and economics, and he surrounded himself with young (most of them in their thirties or early forties) whiz kids who boasted degrees from Yale, MIT, Princeton, and Stanford, and whose brashness and confidence often exceeded their wisdom. Salinas proved to be a dynamic, energetic, and persuasive leader, tirelessly traveling around the country in his signature windbreaker and loafers to preside over a plethora of ceremonial occasions with a dynamism that earned him the nickname "the atomic ant."

Salinas's immediate predecessor, Miguel de la Madrid, had begun economic reforms in earnest by privatizing, deregulating, and generally "liberalizing" the Mexican economy. He had brought Mexico into the General Agreement on Tariffs and Trade (GATT) in 1986, a clear signal that the old days of hermetic, top-down development were over and that Mexico intended to open its economy to the world. But while De la Madrid had often seemed a reluctant reformer, Salinas was a true believer. Although at the start of his presidency he insisted he had no interest in seeking any sort of trade deal with the United States and Canada, once he committed to that notion it became a veritable obsession. To pave the way, Salinas carried out the most radical reforms Mexico had seen since its epic revolution eight decades earlier, a whirlwind of privatization, deregulation, and liberalization that was soon being dubbed

"Salinastroika," in homage to the economic reforms that had brought an end to the Soviet Union.

One of the chief problems with Salinas's economic reforms was that there was no corresponding "Glasnost," or political opening. In his governing style, Salinas was as authoritarian, intolerant, and secretive as any of his predecessors in the Mexican presidency. Although he appointed young ivy-leaguers to his economic team, he entrusted political operations to Fernando Gutiérrez Barrios, a man described by a pair of *New York Times* reporters as the PRI's "darkest prince," with a long history of meting out extreme brutality toward leftist dissenters.[1] During Salinas's six years in office, some 250 activists with the rival party, the PRD, were mysteriously assassinated; Salinas managed to appoint 60 percent of all state governors; and only a small handful of people were privy to government decision-making. Political reform would have to wait. For now, the goal was the same one that had been pursued by generations of Mexican leaders – remaking Mexico into a modern, "first world" country.

Salinas began negotiating the North American Free Trade Agreement (NAFTA) – or the Tratado de Libre Comercio (TLC), as it was known in Mexico – in 1990. For years, debate about the TLC was daily front-page news in Mexico's papers, and the promises made on the agreement's behalf – which happened to coincide with a bout of solid and sustained economic growth in Mexico in the early 1990s – allowed Mexicans to indulge in a rare moment of optimism. Middle-class Mexicans used credit cards to purchase foreign products whose prices were held down by an overvalued peso. The economy grew at a very respectable rate, inflation was brought under control, exports rose sevenfold between 1984 and 1994, and the deficit was reduced to nearly nothing. For the poor, Salinas launched a program called "Solidarity," which provided some $18 billion for such projects as electrification, paving streets, building or repairing school buildings, and upgrading hospitals. To Americans, who were once again ratcheting up their anti-immigration rhetoric, Salinas boldly promised that NAFTA would solve the immigration problem definitively, that Mexico would soon be exporting its goods instead of its people.

Had time somehow stopped in 1993, Carlos Salinas de Gortari would surely have gone down in history as one of Mexico's most effective leaders. He was hailed internationally as an eminent statesman, and the

United States enthusiastically backed his candidacy to head the World Trade Organization once his presidency ended. But unfortunately, behind all the good cheer lurked some grim realities. The Solidarity program, although it was quite popular among poor Mexicans, had virtually no impact in reducing poverty, and the charge that it was intended mainly as a vote getter for the PRI was entirely plausible. And, as usual, the benefits of economic growth were unequally distributed: the share of national wealth going to the poor and middle class declined, while the rich once again got richer. Some Mexicans did very well indeed: when Salinas sold off the national telephone service, the purchaser – Carlos Slim Helú – was en route to becoming one of the world's top billionaires.

Middle-class people spent lavishly, but they neglected savings. Mexico ran a large current accounts deficit, meaning that it was buying more than it was selling, and the difference was made up by foreign investors who eagerly placed their money in the Mexican stock market. Most economists were aware that the peso was overvalued, and that it was overvalued at least partly because Salinas and his advisors were reluctant to risk devaluation in the run-up to both the passage of NAFTA and the presidential elections. The US government continued to shower praise on Salinas and to describe the Mexican economy as "fundamentally strong," even though US officials were well aware of the peso's precarious state.[2]

Meanwhile, Mexico and its soon-to-be free trading partners were glibly ignoring the fact that Mexico was in no condition to enter a trade agreement as an equal partner with the United States and Canada. Not only was Mexico's economy smaller, poorer, and more unequal than those of the United States and Canada, but Mexico was plagued by many other internal problems that boded ill for the success of the venture. Despite some modest political reforms by the Salinas government – such as, for the first time, placing elections in the hands of an electoral commission instead of having them overseen by the official party – Mexico continued to have an authoritarian and corrupt political system that suffered from a critical lack of transparency. Mexico also continued to have a troubled relationship with the rule of law. A 2002 United Nations report stirred up considerable controversy when it declared that "corrupt practices" affected more than half of the justice system, and that in some states civil matters could not be resolved without the payment of a bribe. There was no trial by jury or open argument, judges did not have to explain their decisions to defendants, and the entire system was notoriously politicized.[3] At another level, police were not paid a living wage, and they routinely supplemented their incomes through extortion and collaboration in criminal enterprises.

The fruits of Mexico's wealth were not only unevenly distributed among social classes, but they were also concentrated to an alarming degree in a handful of regions. Roughly half of the country's economic activity took place in Mexico City and in the states of Mexico, Nuevo León, and Jalisco, while 25 out of its 32 states accounted for less than 3 percent of domestic production. Unemployment and underemployment were endemic in the impoverished southern states. By the 1990s those states had joined the traditional "sending states" of the north-central region in providing large numbers of migrants to the United States. They were joined by Central Americans who streamed across Mexico's southern border, giving Mexico an immigration crisis of its own. NAFTA not only contained nothing that might have eased the regional disparities, but it promised to exacerbate them by giving advantages to the northern tier of states, which had easy access to the US market.

Mexico's educational system also left much to be desired. The average length of schooling for Mexicans was seven years, which compared unfavorably not only to the averages in more developed countries, but also to countries with comparable levels of economic development. Initiatives in education, healthcare, and wealth redistribution could not readily be undertaken given that Mexico continued to collect taxes that amounted to only 11 percent of gross domestic product, a level that was low even by Latin American standards (to put this in perspective, the United States collected 34 percent of GDP at the time, while Brazil was at 37 percent). And Mexico's agricultural policies continued to be heavily skewed in favor of well-heeled agribusiness operations. NAFTA promised to eliminate tariffs on corn imports from the United States and Canada within 15 years of its enactment, and when that happened it was a foregone conclusion that the country's remaining small-scale corn farmers would be wiped out once and for all.

Given the stark disparities among the signatories of NAFTA, the exalted expectations for it were unlikely to be fulfilled. Even so, the

Mexican people can hardly have been prepared for the series of rude shocks that erupted in 1994, the year the trade agreement went into effect. On January 1 of that year, the very day NAFTA formally became a reality, Indians in the impoverished southern state of Chiapas rose up in arms, in a movement that called itself the Zapatista Army of National Liberation. Connecting themselves symbolically to the peasant movement led by Emiliano Zapata during the Mexican Revolution of 1910, the Zapatistas denounced NAFTA as a scheme to further enrich the already rich, and to further impoverish and marginalize the poor, especially the indigenous poor.

Then in March, Luis Donaldo Colosio, Salinas's handpicked successor to the presidency, was assassinated while campaigning in the city of Tijuana. It was the highest-level political assassination in Mexico since 1928, and it came as a terrible jolt to Mexicans. It also jolted foreign investors, who, sensing serious political instability in the offing, began to pull their capital out of the country. On September 28, another political assassination rocked the nation. This time the victim was José Francisco Ruiz Massieu, the second highest official in the PRI. Adding to the shock, investigators announced that they had discovered a link between the Ruiz Massieu murder and Raúl Salinas de Gortari, brother of the President.

With each new shock, more foreign capital fled the country. Mexico had been steadily depleting its foreign reserves to prop up the overvalued peso, and as payment came due it was increasingly apparent that the overvalued peso was a severe liability. Carlos Salinas left office without devaluing the peso, boasting that he was the first Mexican president in 30 years to avoid such a move. But in December, only three weeks after Salinas's departure, his successor allowed the peso to float. It immediately lost 20 percent of its value and continued a precipitous decline.

The impact was devastating. Mexicans had become heavily dependent on imports for food and basic consumer goods, the prices of which shot up alarmingly. Many middle-class Mexicans found themselves unable to make payments on overextended credit cards; many more lost their jobs and their homes. Thousands of businesses failed, and more than a million people found themselves suddenly unemployed. Mexico was plunged into its most severe economic crisis since the 1930s. And even though the United States and international lenders came through with some $50 billion in bailout funds that Mexico was able to repay by 1997, ahead of schedule, the Mexican economy had been dealt a serious blow from which is has not yet recovered.

In 1995 Mexico experienced a horrendous crime wave, with robberies and kidnappings spiking to unprecedented heights. By 1998, "public insecurity" had replaced the ailing economy as the public's chief concern. Many middle-class people, faced with catastrophic debt, formed a militant, albeit non-violent, protest movement that quickly spread throughout the country. Demoralization took a toll, as people who had been led to anticipate a bright and prosperous future woke up to realize that Mexico's supposedly imminent enrichment had been a cruel illusion, a classic bubble that had burst spectacularly.

Resurgent Nativism in the United States

By the early 1990s the unintended consequences of the Immigration Reform and Control Act (IRCA) were becoming apparent. Although illegal immigration from Mexico to the United States dropped by nearly 40 percent in the years immediately after IRCA went into effect in 1987, by the early 1990s Mexicans had discovered that they had little to fear from the stepped-up border enforcement or from employer sanctions. Employers were allowed the massive loophole of merely having to demonstrate a "good faith" effort to examine a job applicant's documents, while they had no obligation to verify those documents' authenticity. Efforts to create a more secure identification system were denounced by civil rights advocates as an invasion of privacy that would inevitably lead to a national ID system, so that idea was scrapped. The predictable result was a boom in the production and marketing of counterfeit documents. Beyond that, the Reagan and Bush administrations, both of which opposed government regulation in principle, showed little interest in enforcing the employer sanctions. They consistently underfunded the Departments of Labor and Justice, which were tasked with enforcing the sanctions. The number of INS agents dedicated to enforcement of employer sanctions was cut by half between 1989 and 1994, and the number of fines imposed on employers declined by the same amount. By 1999 only 2 percent of the INS budget was devoted to checking up on employers, which meant that there were only 340 full-time INS staffers detailed to inspect every job site in the United States.

Nor did the INS devote its energies to ensuring that employers who hired illegal immigrants provide a decent working environment. In the California garment industry, which employed large numbers of undocumented immigrants, half of all employers paid less than the minimum wage, few paid overtime, and some 93 percent violated health and safety regulations, yet employers faced no consequences for such transgressions. Instead of punishing employers, the INS focused its attention resolutely on building up border enforcement, though this did little to impede the flow of undocumented immigrants into the country.

Other fallout from IRCA was also becoming apparent by the early 1990s. The 3 million people whose status had been regularized by IRCA were now able to bring spouses and dependents to the United States under the preference system, and many encouraged relatives and friends who were *not* eligible for such preferences to enter illegally. So, once the shock of IRCA dissipated, the law's impact was, ironically, to *increase* Mexican immigration, both legal and illegal. By 2000 there were four times as many Mexicans living in the United States as there had been prior to the passage of IRCA. By that time, Hispanics had become the nation's largest minority.

IRCA also had the effect of lowering wages and worsening working conditions for low-skilled workers, while decreasing tax collection. Employers were stuck with the increased costs of at least going through the motions of complying with IRCA's provisions – which entailed certifying that they had examined a prospective worker's documents and filling out an I-9 form – and many compensated for those costs by slashing wages. Some employers took to hiring workers through subcontractors, who would compensate themselves for their services by withholding a portion of the workers' pay. Others did their hiring off the books entirely, paying workers in cash. Employers who used such informal arrangements seldom deducted taxes and did not necessarily feel themselves bound by occupational health and safety regulations or minimum wages laws. These trends were not restricted only to undocumented workers, but to much of the unskilled workforce, which saw an across the board decline in wages of 21 cents a year between 1986 and 1992.

The mid-1990s witnessed a fairly sudden spike in anti-immigrant sentiment that probably exceeded all earlier such outbursts in its vehemence. This likely had much to do with trends in the US economy that had been apparent since the late 1970s. In 1965 US corporations enjoyed an average rate of profit of 10 percent; by the late 1970s the rate of profit had declined by half, clearly signaling an end to the post-World War II economic boom brought on by a rise in global competition. Corporations sought to compensate for declining profitability by slashing jobs or moving their operations offshore. The hemorrhaging of manufacturing jobs led to a rise in unemployment, a drop in real wages, and an increased prevalence of "contingent" workers – that is, workers who were hired part time or for short stints, and who had no job security. Undocumented immigrants were well suited to this rising demand for contingent workers, and they responded to the call in huge numbers.

The motor force of the US economy shifted from manufacturing to finance, meaning that speculators and investors now made the important decisions and reaped the big profits. The economy showed growth even while household median income declined and the gap between rich and poor widened. At the same time, the Reagan administration cut taxes even while drastically increasing spending on defense, causing the national debt to explode and increasing popular anxiety about the future. Reagan himself set the tone by painting government as the enemy and vilifying "welfare queens" who supposedly defrauded taxpayers by collecting enormous sums in government benefits. In this milieu it was perhaps inevitable that a significant portion of the American public came increasingly to scapegoat immigrants for driving up the debt and undermining US prosperity. Even though some highly credible studies concluded that legal and undocumented immigrants paid significantly more in taxes than they collected in social services,[4] polls consistently showed that a majority of Americans were convinced that the opposite was the case.

Ground zero for the rise in immigrant bashing was California, which, in addition to the general trends just discussed, had experienced rapid and dramatic changes in the composition of its population since the

1970s. California's foreign-born population rose from being only 9 percent of the total in 1960, to 22 percent in 1990. California was the destination for one in four immigrants to the United States, and more immigrants had arrived there during the 1980s than during the previous three decades combined. Los Angeles County saw an even greater concentration of new arrivals, with a third of its population made up of immigrants. In fact, by the 1990s immigrants and their offspring had come to account for virtually all of California's population increase.

As early as 1984, California voters had approved a ballot initiative opposing multilingual ballots that had been mandated by Congress, and in 1986 the state had adopted a measure making English the state's sole official language. But the more concerted anti-immigrant push came in the early 1990s, when the state's real estate bubble burst and military spending dipped, sending California's economy into severe recession. Pete Wilson, a former San Diego mayor and two-term Republican US senator, was elected governor in 1990, and he was quick to recognize the political potential of anti-immigrant sentiment.

The anti-immigration movement was given an added boost in early 1992, when San Diego Border Patrol chief Gustavo de la Viña stationed extra Border Patrol agents and new detection equipment at one of the border's busiest crossing points to intercept Mexican immigrants returning from Christmas trips to Mexico. The border closure channeled virtually all of the immigrants toward a single, narrow crossing point, where they quickly discovered that their most promising option was to cross en masse in the hope of overwhelming Border Patrol agents. People began crossing in groups of 50 or more, then they would disperse onto Interstate 5, snarling traffic and causing general consternation. De la Viña videotaped some of these so-called "banzai runs" and released the tapes with the provocative title, *Border Under Siege*, which clearly aimed to send the message that the chaos of the banzai runs was business as usual at the San Diego crossing.

The Los Angeles riots of April and May 1992, while ostensibly sparked by the acquittal of police officers implicated in the beating of an African-American man, were also a violent eruption of ethnic tensions, wherein both Asian and Hispanic immigrants were targeted. Such violent and disorderly episodes reinforced Californians' sense that their state was changing in profound and irrevocable ways that they were helpless to forestall. Pete Wilson saw the immigration issue as an important key to his reelection hopes.

In August 1993 Governor Wilson published an open letter to President Bill Clinton wherein he claimed that the use of schools, hospitals, and welfare by illegal immigrants was costing California – whose public finances were already in disarray, though largely for reasons that had little to do with illegal immigration – some $1.5 billion a year. He demanded sweeping measures against illegal immigration, including the repeal of the clause in the Fourteenth Amendment of the US Constitution granting US citizenship to persons born in the United States.

Soon after, a group of ten people circulated a petition to introduce a sweeping ballot initiative against illegal immigration. The petition soon garnered over 385,000 signatures. Thus was born the so-called Save Our State (SOS) initiative, better known as Proposition 187. Bankrolled by the state Republican Party, Proposition 187 ostensibly aimed to introduce radical reforms. It would deny all social services, including public education and all non-emergency healthcare, to undocumented immigrants. Schools would have to verify the immigration status of their students and their students' parents, while service providers would be required to report suspected undocumented immigrants to the INS and California's attorney general. Proposition 187 would also have made the manufacture, distribution, or use of false documents a felony. In order to make Proposition 187 immune from political tampering, the California legislature would not be allowed to amend it "except to further its purposes," and then only by a supermajority vote in both houses or by another voter referendum. Interestingly, the initiative would not have explicitly made it a crime to hire undocumented workers, nor did it include any mention of penalties for employers who violated the provisions of the IRCA legislation.

The supporters of Proposition 187 were well aware that what they were proposing was sure to be struck down by the courts. Voters were not led to believe that the law would make any real difference, but they were instead told that a "yes" vote would "send a message" to Washington that Californians were angry and wanted serious government action on the immigration issue. The campaigning was fierce, both for and against the Act. Finally, in the voting of November 1994, Californians approved

Proposition 187 by 59 percent, with 41 percent voting no. Pete Wilson was reelected as governor by a comfortable margin.

Proposition 187's practical impact was minimal, for, as expected, the courts quickly ruled its provisions unconstitutional. The Supreme Court case *Plyler v. Doe* of 1982 had established the principle that the children of illegal immigrants could not be denied public education, so the voters of California would have needed action by the national Congress to get their way (action that some legislators attempted, and failed, to carry out in a 1996 immigration bill).

But Proposition 187's failure to become law did not mean that it failed to have a profound impact, although some of its consequences were the opposite of what its champions intended. Proposition 187 helped to transform the politics of California by bringing a host of new actors onto the political stage. Since immigrants in general, and Latinos in particular, were the primary target of the legislation, not surprisingly the initiative led to a massive mobilization on the part of Hispanic and immigrants' rights groups. Latino participation in politics, which had been practically non-existent before 1994, began to become an important force. The Republican Party in California, which was principally identified with the anti-immigration movement, paid a steep price at the polls. The growing hostility toward immigrants in California encouraged many immigrants to seek their fortunes elsewhere, becoming a factor in creating the new geography of Mexican immigration.

Proposition 187 was not the only episode of the mid-1990s that thrust the issue of illegal immigration onto the national consciousness. In September 1993 Silvestre Reyes, Border Patrol chief at El Paso, Texas, undertook a bold experiment he dubbed "Operation Blockade" (later changed to "Operation Hold-the-Line"). Responding to citizens' complaints about illegal immigrants traipsing across their properties and through their neighborhoods, as well as to a lawsuit brought by residents of an El Paso Mexican-American neighborhood who complained of being harassed by Border Patrol agents who took them for illegals, Reyes developed a strategy that came to be known as "prevention through deterrence." Instead of trying to detect and arrest illegal immigrants after they had entered the country, Reyes's idea was simply to mass Border Patrol agents in the most popular crossing spots, with helicopter assistance, to prevent immigrants from crossing in the first place. The strategic placement of agents was soon supplemented by a new fence that stretched across the western reaches of the city. The new tactic worked quite well, as least in accomplishing its stated purpose: immigrants were forced to cross the border in out-of-the-way stretches of desert – "hostile terrain," in Border Patrol parlance. Although many El Paso residents found the fence objectionable, the essential effort was quite popular, for it deflected immigration to places where it went on unseen, even while cutting down on the harassment of El Paso citizens.

Although Operation Hold-the-Line mostly deflected, rather than stopped, illegal immigration, it was popular enough to win Silvestre Reyes a seat in the US House of Representatives. It also attracted the attention of national politicians, including President Bill Clinton and Attorney General Janet Reno, who began to lavish funding on the Immigration and Naturalization Service. The INS's budget for border enforcement doubled from $400 million for fiscal year 1993 to $800 million in fiscal year 1997, while the numbers of Border Patrol agents also doubled. The administration devoted special attention to the border's most frequented crossing point, the San Diego sector. Between 1994 and 1998 the number of Border Patrol agents guarding that sector went from 980 to 2,264; the length of fencing from 19 to 45 miles; and the number of underground sensors from 448 to 1,214. Directly influenced by Reyes's Operation Hold-the-Line, the San Diego buildup was dubbed "Operation Gatekeeper." Supplementing the new agents, fences, and sensors, high-intensity floodlights were trained on the border crossing both day and night, and a variety of high-tech gadgets (infrared scopes, motion detectors, trip wires) was deployed. Gatekeeper brought calm to the formerly chaotic stretch of border, ending the nightly spectacle of "banzai runs" into the teeming traffic of I-5. Operations Hold-the-Line and Gatekeeper were so successful at creating the comforting illusion of control that they were soon joined by similar operations in Nogales, Arizona, and south Texas.

The growing mania for border enforcement clearly responded to political imperatives rather than practical concerns. Since the 1980s the American public had been sold on the notion that the United States had "lost control of its borders." Politicians feared being painted as soft on immigration, and since the southern border was the most visible point of entry, it became the preferred stage for political performance.

Operations like Hold-the-Line and Gatekeeper brought a semblance of order and tranquility to some sections of the border, especially those abutted by populous cities. More Border Patrol agents and new technologies made it possible to increase the numbers of apprehensions of undocumented entrants, and such statistics were given ample publicity. Other statistics showing that the increased border enforcement had no effect on the numbers of undocumented immigrants crossing into the United States – or indeed, that illegal immigration was steadily increasing, despite the border buildup – were downplayed. It scarcely mattered that as many as half of illegal immigrants in the United States never crossed the border, instead entering the country legally and allowing their visas to expire. It also hardly mattered that "internal enforcement" of immigration laws – sanctions against employers of undocumented immigrants and enforcement of workplace standards on health, safety, and wages – was almost entirely neglected. The border buildup was undoubtedly popular with the American people, who found in it some reassurance that the government was acting with toughness and resolve to confront illegal immigration. As with the case of the "war on drugs" – where longstanding policies have a similar record of being ineffective and counterproductive – actually resolving the immigration problem was less important than staging high-profile acts of political theater.

This is not to say that the border buildup has had no consequences. It made border crossing more dangerous and expensive – the average price of the services of a *coyote*, or people smuggler, rose sharply and rapidly, from $189 on average in 1990, to $482 in 1998, to $1,500 by 2009, with some special services going for $3,000 and $5,000. As crossing became more dangerous, people-smuggling grew more lucrative. *Coyotes* became more professional and sophisticated. Small timers were forced out of the business, and smuggling came increasingly to be dominated by about a dozen family based syndicates who were able to provide state-of-the-art services in exchange for hefty fees. They were skilled enough to ensure that most of those who sought to cross into the United States were successful.

For those who did successfully cross into the United States, the increased danger and expense that re-entering the United States now entailed made them disinclined to leave, as previous generations of migrants had routinely done. The beefed-up border enforcement thus helped to convert what had been a circular migration into migration of a far more settled and permanent sort. The new immigrants who put down solid roots created bases for new settlements in parts of the country that had not been accustomed to the presence of Mexicans. The expanded border controls – especially in the San Diego sector, which had long been the most popular crossing place – diverted border crossers to new, more remote crossing spots, increasing geographical dispersion. Also in the 1990s, the California economy slumped even as hostility toward immigrants grew more heated, encouraging many Mexicans to leave for other climes. So Mexican immigration, which had always been heavily concentrated in the southwestern states and Illinois, now became a national phenomenon, with Mexican immigrant colonies expanding in the Southeast, Northeast, and Midwest. By the early 1990s nearly a third of all Mexican immigrants were going to places other than the traditional destinations, and they were no longer associated so exclusively with agriculture and the service industries. Many found work in meatpacking and poultry plants, seafood canneries, commercial and residential construction, and many other sectors that had traditionally seen little participation from Mexican immigrants. They were aided by the pattern of economic growth in the United States during the 1990s and the first years of the twenty-first century, which tended toward greater polarization of the workforce, with more and more workers performing low-paid, low-skilled jobs.

The border buildup did not discourage immigrants, but it did force them to find new crossing points in "hostile terrain," isolated and dangerous stretches of desert or mountain. The average numbers of people who died trying to cross into the United States roughly doubled after 1995. According to figures compiled by Mexican officials, deaths at the border rose from 87 in 1996 to 499 in 2000. Most died of exposure and thirst, though killings by bandits, smugglers, and drug traffickers have become more common.

In fact, recently the smuggling of illegal drugs and the smuggling of people have become increasingly intertwined, adding considerably to the dangers of border crossing. Powerful and ruthless drug cartels either run people-smuggling operations directly, or they force the people-smugglers to pay them taxes, usually of about $110 per migrant. Smugglers who refuse to pay, or who underreport the numbers of migrants they are transporting, risk violent retribution. And the migrants themselves must also deal with new dangers. According to David Kyle, a sociology professor at the University of California-Davis:

> A migrant has historically calculated risk by considering the classic dangers of random crime and the desert environment. Those aren't so different than the risks against him in Mexico, so they can be rationalized. But not criminal syndicates. The nature of that risk is probably unacceptable to most, because the fear isn't that they just go after you, but that if you cross them, they are powerful enough to go after your whole family, your whole village.[5]

Border enforcement is by no means the only anti-immigration initiative pursued during the past two decades. The Clinton administration's approach to immigration issues was heavily shaped by the Republican Party, which took control of the US Congress in 1994. Touting their "Contract with America," the Republicans hoped to dismantle much of the welfare state that had been built up since the 1930s. Representatives Lamar Smith (R-TX) and Elton Gallegly (R-CA) made concerted efforts to bring to the national stage some of the initiatives that had undergirded Proposition 187, including denying the children of undocumented immigrants access to citizenship and education.

Debates surrounding such proposals revealed the serious internal rifts that immigration policy represented for the Republican Party, which claimed to represent law and order and the preservation of primordial Americanness, but which also championed business and free market capitalism. There was an unavoidable tension between preserving the nation's ethnic makeup and upholding the law, while at the same time ensuring business relatively unfettered access to low-cost labor. Strange bedfellows – not an uncommon phenomenon in the history of immigration policy-making – began to appear. In the Senate, for example, conservative Utah Republican Orrin Hatch joined Massachusetts liberal Democrat Ted Kennedy in urging the repeal of employer sanctions. House majority leader Newt Gingrich initially backed Lamar Smith's bill, but changed his mind after meeting with representatives of the fast food and chain restaurant industries. Some Republican Party leaders were also aware of the growing clout of Hispanic voters, who would surely be alienated by too harsh and punitive a stance on immigration issues.

The bill that eventually emerged from conference was titled the Illegal Immigration Reform and Immigrant Responsibility Act of 1996 (IIRIRA), which was signed by President Clinton on September 30, 1996. It did not contain the so-called Gallegly amendment denying public education to undocumented immigrants, but it did contain several restrictive measures: civil and criminal penalties for illegal entry into the United States were increased, the ability of immigrants to challenge INS decisions in court was limited, provisions were made for "expedited removal" of undesirable immigrants, state and local governments were authorized to deny public benefits to both illegal and legal immigrants, and any legal resident attempting to sponsor the immigration of a family member would be obliged to support that family at a level at least 125 percent of the official poverty line. The Act also included yet another round of stepped-up funding for the Border Patrol, which was to have 10,000 officers by 2001, and for various border-monitoring technologies.

Coming around the same time as the IIRIRA was the Personal Responsibility and Work Opportunity Reconciliation Act of 1996, better known as the Clinton-era "welfare reform." The act reiterated that undocumented immigrants were ineligible for federal, state, and local public benefits, while it barred even legal immigrants from getting food stamps or other "means tested" benefits.

Once again, unintended consequences ensued. Historically, legal Mexican immigrants had shown little interest in acquiring United States citizenship. The punitive measures in the 1996 bills now inspired many immigrants to pursue citizenship, and – understanding that the new citizens would overwhelmingly vote for Democratic Party candidates – the Clinton administration was happy to lend a hand. Vice President Al Gore was detailed to head up a program called "Citizenship USA," which streamlined the process for acquiring citizenship, cutting wait time from two years to six months. Applications for new citizenship skyrocketed, from an average of 300,000 prior to 1994 to 1 million in 1996, and a backlog of half a million cases was eliminated. Many of those now applying for citizenship were the same people who had been "amnestied" under the IRCA legislation of 1986.

The spate of new citizens helped to profoundly change the imm-igration equation. During the mobilization for Proposition 187, the prevailing assumption had been that immigrants do not vote. Although Latino and Asian immigrants remained underrepresented at the voting booth, they nevertheless emerged as a force to be reckoned with. By 1996, 72 percent of the Latino vote was going to the Democratic Party, up from 60 percent four years earlier. Immigrant bashing began to look less and less like good political strategy. Perhaps cognizant of this new reality, Congress did a bit of back peddling, restoring social security benefits to many immigrants who had resided in the United States prior to the enactment of the welfare reform law in 1997, and restoring access to food stamps the following year. The courts also managed to soften some of the provisions of the 1996 Acts.

There remained a hard core of anti-immigration activists in the United States, and most continued to find a home in the Republican Party. There were also some very prominent anti-immigration activists outside of government, perhaps most famously journalist Peter Brimelow – himself an immigrant from the UK – whose 1995 book *Alien Nation* became a modest bestseller. Waxing nostalgic for the days prior to 1965 – the year that Congress abolished the national origins quotas and the United States had begun to admit large numbers of Asians, Latinos, and Africans – Brimelow warned of a catastrophe in the offing. Predominantly non-white immigrants would cause a population boom that would out-strip US resources, degrade the environment, bankrupt the nation, destroy its cultural fabric, and subvert its political system. While Brimelow's work seemed clearly intended more to frighten than enlighten, and although most of its claims were roundly debunked by more thoughtful writers,[6] he nevertheless remains a commanding presence on the far right fringes of American politics, which have proved their attention-getting capabilities beyond doubt. Brimelow's recommenda-tions – that all immigration to the United States be halted at once, and that the Republican Party should concentrate its efforts on getting "white votes" – are not likely to be taken very seriously in policy-making circles. Still, Brimelow has more recently been joined by a number of others in politics and the media whose views and prescriptions are at least as provocative.

As for the Republican Party, the political realities of immigration – and the obvious political folly of trying to appeal exclusively to white Americans – have proved difficult. In 2000 the party chose as its candidate Texas Governor George W. Bush, whose stance on immigration was uncharacteristically mild and flexible. Bush, who spoke some Spanish, had Hispanic friends and in-laws, and made much of his affinity for newly elected Mexican President Vicente Fox, seemed the ideal candidate to win over at least a good portion of the Hispanic vote. One of Bush's earliest initiatives, in fact, was to meet with Fox at the latter's Guanajuato hacienda to discuss an ambitious program entailing massive legalization of undocumented immigrants and a new "guest worker" program, goals that had limited appeal within Bush's own party.

The Impact of NAFTA

One reality that made the anti-immigration backlash of the 1990s so odd was that it coincided with the implementation of NAFTA. As migration scholars Douglas Massey, Jorge Durand, and Nolan Malone point out, US policy-makers were apparently guided by the illogical supposition that they could start down the road toward integrating three major economies – which would by definition entail a steep rise in border crossing by people and vehicles and all manner of goods – without generating a corresponding rise in the movement of labor, which, after all, is one of the essential factors in any economy.[7] When Mexican President Carlos Salinas de Gortari began the NAFTA negotiations by trying to persuade American and Canadian officials that opening the borders for trade might call for a relaxation of the laws governing migration among the three countries, he was told in no uncertain terms that any insistence on more open borders would be a sure deal breaker. American negotiators were also able to point out a logical fallacy: if NAFTA fulfilled its promise to bring prosperity to Mexico, then it would solve the immigration problem. There was, therefore, no need to make it an explicit bargaining point.

NAFTA was indeed sold to both the Mexican and American publics with the promise that it would bring prosperity to Mexico – that it would enable Mexico to "export goods instead of people" – without, at the same time, doing any damage to the prosperity of the other two signatory nations. But for the United States and Canada, Mexico held out the traditional lure of low wages and lax regulation. Therein lay a fundamental contradiction of NAFTA: if wages were going to be low enough to attract capital, then it was unlikely that many good, high-paying jobs would be created.

In fact, NAFTA has created few jobs of any kind in Mexico. Defenders of the agreement maintain that, "in its own terms," NAFTA has been a rousing success. Trade among the three partner countries has risen tremendously. Mexican exports to the United States increased at an average annual rate of 14 percent between 1993 and 2002, while US exports to Mexico have increased at an annual rate of 10 percent per year. Foreign Direct Investment (FDI) in Mexico has also expanded from an average of around $4 billion a year before NAFTA to $13 billion a year after. Prior to NAFTA, petroleum accounted for three quarters of Mexico's exports; after NAFTA, 90 percent of Mexico's exports consisted of manufactured goods, and manufacturing productivity has risen by 80 percent. Mexico has become a leading exporter of cars, electronics, and industrial parts, mostly to the United States.

But even NAFTA's defenders admit that the agreement was far from a panacea. Mexico's economic growth was a fairly sluggish 3 percent per year, even before the terrible recession of 2009 put it into negative territory. More importantly, job creation has been slow, poverty has not decreased, and the volume of migration to the United States has increased, from 370,000 per year on average between 1990 and 1994 to 575,000 per year between 2000 and 2004. This has much to do with unwise domestic policies within Mexico. But it also owes something to the fact that the agreement never envisioned real equality among the three signatory countries. Vicente Fox, who was elected President of Mexico in 2000, praised NAFTA even while gingerly chiding US policy-makers by saying that "I don't think we have come to an understanding yet of what it means to be partners, or to an understanding that partnership is the key to the success of NAFTA."[8]

Statistics showing a dramatic increase in FDI and a sharp increase in Mexico's exports are misleading. Foreign investors used their money, for the most part, to purchase already-existing factories or to buy shares in Mexican enterprises. Seldom did their investments entail an expansion of Mexico's productive capacity, a significant upgrade in technology, or the creation of well-paid jobs. The boom in exports, meanwhile, includes exports from maquiladoras, those foreign-owned plants that import materials duty-free, assemble them, and re-export them to the United States. Since Mexico's only tangible benefit from maquiladora production comes in the form of job creation and value-added taxes, such items do not qualify as real exports. And yet maquiladora production accounted for about half of all of Mexico's exports of manufactured goods, and about half of all the jobs created in Mexico, between 1993 and 1998. The sector expanded by 30 percent between 1994 and 2000, more than any other sector of the Mexican economy.

The boom in the maquiladora sector has had its share of baneful effects. The wages the maquiladoras paid were only one and a half times the Mexican minimum wage, which in turn was about half the average manufacturing wage in Mexico. Maquiladora management took great pains to prevent the formation of unions, and indeed confessed that the lack of unions was a big part of what made Mexico an attractive location for the plants. Mexico has an extremely progressive labor code, but that code routinely goes unenforced. With few protections and little recourse, maquiladora workers were often forced to work overtime without extra pay, were hired and fired at will, and were subject to a variety of abuses. Mexico's environmental protection laws are weaker than those of the United States – another key attraction for manufacturers – and even those weak regulations are routinely honored in the breach. According to one estimate, only 11 percent of all toxic waste generated by the maquiladoras was properly treated, and most of the waste was illegally dumped.[9] And since 2000, even the maquiladora sector itself declined owing to competition from other, mostly Asian, countries where production costs are lower still.

The maquiladoras also worsened the already severe problem of regional disequilibrium within Mexico, for the plants that benefited the most were those that had easy access to the American market – that is, those close to the northern border. The northern border became relatively prosperous while those parts of the country farthest from the border – especially the southern states of Puebla, Veracruz, Oaxaca, Guerrero, and Chiapas – languished. While historically those states had sent few migrants to the United States, now they were sending significant numbers.

Outside of the maquiladora sector, few new jobs were created. About half of the non-agricultural jobs created since NAFTA went into effect are in what is euphemistically classified as "microbusinesses" – that is, firms with five or fewer employees. This category contains "self-employed" individuals, including, for example, people who eek out a bare living by selling chewing gum on the sidewalk. Employment in this sector is notoriously unstable and seldom comes with benefits.

Another unfortunate impact of NAFTA, of course, was to link Mexico's economy much more closely to that of the United States. Mexico has long been extremely vulnerable to economic downturns in the United States, but that vulnerability was greatly amplified by NAFTA, which reoriented the country's economy toward production for export. That problem became glaringly apparent with the great recession of 2008–2009.

Mexican Immigration in the National Security Era

President George W. Bush used his moderate position on immigration reform and his supposed affinity for Mexican President Vicente Fox to court the Hispanic vote, with some success. Unfortunately, once in office Bush seemed tepid and confused on immigration matters, torn between his oft-stated commitment to immigration reform and placating the right wing of the Republican Party.

Vicente Fox might well have proved a useful ally. His election to the presidency was undoubtedly historic, since he was a member of the conservative National Action Party (PAN) rather than the Institutional Revolutionary Party (PRI), which had exercised near-total control of Mexican politics since 1928. His election was rightly hailed as a milestone in the development of democracy in Mexico, but his term also demonstrated amply that democracy is no more a panacea for what ails Mexico than free trade. Plagued by an opposition-controlled Congress and a vacillating and lackluster leadership style, Fox made little progress toward correcting Mexico's many weaknesses, particularly the low levels of tax collection and the abysmal education system. Congress, which had long acted as a rubber stamp for the powerful presidents of the PRI, now took to asserting itself at Fox's expense, stymieing needed reforms at every turn.

Fox seems to have been genuinely committed to effecting sweeping immigration reform. Perhaps a measure of his seriousness regarding the immigration issue was his appointment of Jorge Castañeda as Foreign Minister. Castañeda, a one-time leftist intellectual who had moved increasingly to the center, had a longstanding interest in migration and considerable expertise and experience in US–Mexican relations. Moreover, the timing seemed ripe for serious binational negotiations on migration. The economic changes of the 1980s and 1990s had created enormous demand for low-wage, low-skilled labor in the United States. Organized labor, which had seen its membership and influence decline over the course of several decades, had come to see immigration less as a threat to American workers than as a potential pool of workers ripe for the organizing. The transition to democracy in Mexico had generated a tide of goodwill in the United States. And the election of George W. Bush, a purported friend to Mexico and advocate of immigration reform, added further to the optimism. Bush's first foreign trip as President was to Mexico, and Vicente Fox was the first official foreign guest welcomed to the United States in Bush's first term.

Adding still further to the sense of optimism and opportunity was the report of a joint task force organized by the Carnegie Endowment for International Peace and the International Relations Faculty of the Autonomous Technological Institute of Mexico, issued in 2001. The report, titled "Mexico–US Migration: A Shared Responsibility," envisioned the migration problem as a binational issue in need of binational solutions. The report proposed a program for "comprehensive" reform, which included a large increase in the availability of legal visas for Mexican workers, a cooperative effort to crack down on illegal smuggling and save lives at dangerous border crossings, opportunities for Mexican immigrants in the United States to regularize their status, and programs to create jobs in the prime sending regions in Mexico. The report appeared to be a workable blueprint for meaningful reforms, a notion that was given added credence after meetings between Bush and Fox in February and April 2001. Joint statements issued after those meetings called for "formal high-level negotiations aimed at achieving short- and long-term agreements that will allow us to constructively address migration and labor issues between our two countries."[10]

After those preliminary meetings in February and April, Fox came to Washington to plead for a "regularization" of the status of undocumented Mexicans who had been living and paying taxes in the United States, and for greater freedom of movement across a more open border. Like many Mexicans, Fox was quick to point out that the wealthier countries of the European Union had invested heavily in building up the economies of the poorer countries – Ireland, Portugal, Spain, Greece, and formerly Soviet countries of Eastern Europe – to ensure greater equality among members; and that open borders among member countries had been written into that agreement.

At the time of Fox's visit, this plan did not seem especially preposterous. Its essential ingredients – legalization and a guest worker program – had the backing of Democrats in Congress, as well as support from a surprising alliance of the AFL-CIO and the US Chamber of Commerce. Fox made the rounds of the media and addressed Congress, confidently predicting that an immigration reform program would be passed before the end of 2001.

Fox's timing could not possibly have been worse. His state visit to Washington came in the first week of September 2001, just days before the terrorist attacks on the World Trade Center and the Pentagon. Although none of the September 11 hijackers came into the United States across the southern border, the attacks led to an obsessive focus on that border, a renewed sense of alarm about American vulnerabilities, and a ferocious turn toward unilateralism on the part of the Bush administration. President Fox's dream of a more open border was among the unsung casualties of that day.

What little remained of the international goodwill that characterized the first months of 2001 was lost irrevocably in 2002 and 2003. Mexico, which held a seat on the United Nations Security Council between 2002 and 2004, firmly opposed the Bush administration's planned invasion of Iraq, effectively scuttling US efforts to get a majority of the Security Council to endorse that invasion. Fox had already become bitterly disillusioned with the Bush administration, which he believed was duplicitous and unreliable. The dispute over the invasion of Iraq made cooperation between the United States and Mexico almost inconceivable for the remainder of Bush's tenure.

The southern border was temporarily shut down in the days after the September 11 attacks, and for several weeks border traffic slowed to a crawl, with four and five hour waits routine. National security became an all-consuming obsession. In October 2001 Bush signed the "Uniting and Strengthening America by Providing Appropriate Tools Required to Intercept and Obstruct Terrorism Act," better known as the USA PATRIOT Act, which, among many other things, allowed for the rapid deportation without a hearing of any alien that the attorney general believed might be a potential terrorist. In early 2002 Congress once again bumped up funding for the Immigration and Naturalization Service, but then early the next year it dissolved the INS altogether, transferring most of its functions to Immigration and Customs Enforcement (ICE) within the newly created Department of Homeland Security (DHS).

Wall and fence building at the border, already much in vogue during the 1990s, now became an even more serious growth industry. In November 2005, DHS announced the Secure Border Initiative (SBI), which committed the United States to increasing the number of border agents, increasing the number of ICE investigators, expanding detention facilities, upgrading detection technologies at the border, increasing border "infrastructure" (i.e., more walls and fences), and increasing "interior" enforcement (i.e., enforcing employer sanctions). In December of the same year the House of Representatives passed the Border Protection, Antiterrorism, and Illegal Immigration Control Act, better known as the Sensenbrenner bill in honor of its chief sponsor, James Sensenbrenner (R-Wis), which mandated 700 miles of "security fencing" at the most frequented border crossing sites. The Sensenbrenner bill did not pass the Senate and never became law, but that did little to dampen the ardor for more fencing. In October 2006 President Bush signed the Secure Fence Act, which ordered the construction of 850 miles of double-layer, reinforced fencing on certain stretches of the southern border; and in 2008 the Bush administration ordered the DHS to complete 370 miles of fencing and 300 miles of vehicle barriers by the end of the year.

Fencing continues to be expensive, controversial, and of very limited effectiveness. The cost of building walls and fences has risen in the past few years from around $3.5 million a mile to $6.5 million; in some especially difficult stretches of wild border topography the cost could reach $16 million per mile. When the cost of maintaining the fences is added, the price tag for the projected 850 miles of fencing could range upwards of $59.5 billion over the course of 25 years. Meanwhile, the Boeing Corporation was awarded an $860 million contract to build a much-touted "virtual fence" – essentially, cameras and radars mounted on tall poles – but a $20 million prototype for that virtual fence built southwest of Tucson, Arizona, was found to be so ineffective that it was scrapped. According to *Defense News*, the technology for the virtual fence "can't tell a terrorist from a tumbleweed."[11] Funding for the expanded Border Patrol – fences being of little use without someone to patrol them – must be added to that cost. As of 2007, that budget was $2.7 billion. The eventual cost of border enforcement will probably be still higher than all of these figures suggest. The estimates for border barricades, for example, do not include labor costs or the expense of acquiring private property that adjoins the border.

Environmentalists also weighed in against the fence builders. A notorious case is that of Smuggler's Gulch, a 230-foot deep canyon near San Diego that, as the name suggests, was long a haven for criminal activity. Contractors working for the US government decapitated a pair of nearby mesas and filled the gulch with nearly 2 million tons – 35,000 truckloads – of dirt, as part of a $60 million project that will eventually include fences and stadium lighting. Environmentalists did their best to stop the project, claiming it would do fatal damage to the Tijuana Estuary, one of the last wetlands ecosystems in southern California and nesting ground for over 370 species of native and migratory birds. The Bush administration, however, gave the DHS explicit authority to disregard local and environmental regulations that might have impeded the construction of this and all other border fencing projects, waiving the Clean Air Act, the Endangered Species Act, Coastal Zone Management, and, for good measure, the National Historic Preservation Act.

So far, the most apparent impact of the barriers has been to drive migrants to more remote and dangerous areas, although some have taken a more assertive approach, attacking the fences with blowtorches and hacksaws, or scaling them with ropes or homemade ladders. According to California Representative Loretta Sanchez, there have been about 3,300 breaches in the San Diego fence, and each repair costs about $1,300. Drug traffickers, meanwhile, have managed to build tunnels under the border. And although it is certain that the border today is more difficult to cross than in the past, the fences have done remarkably little to deter would-be border crossers. Of those who try to get across the southern border, most eventually succeed. So, apart from possibly doing irreparable harm to the environment and causing hundreds of needless deaths, border fencing appears for the most part to be a colossal waste of money.

One major problem, of course, is that virtually unstoppable trends have been moving in precisely opposite directions, practically guaranteeing that border enforcement will be inefficient and ineffective. The trend toward globalization, free trade, and economic integration ensures that the borders will be frenetically busy places, with enormous volumes of traffic. The southern border of the United States, post-NAFTA, is the busiest border in the world, with an average of 222,000 vehicles crossing per day. About 5 million trucks cross each year, carrying goods valued at around $250 billion. The Border Patrol, which is assigned the task of stopping undocumented border crossers, interdicting drugs, and detecting terrorists, increased its size from 2,000 agents in 1986 to 12,200 agents by 2000, its budget swelling from $200 million to nearly $1.5 billion by 2002. Even so, the burgeoning border police force must necessarily let most traffic pass uninspected, relying on nothing more than agent intuition to decide which trucks merit a closer look. Trucks have certainly carried quantities of drugs and undocumented immigrants into the United States, though as yet no documented (or publicized) terrorists.

The anxieties provoked by the September 11 attacks added further fuel to an already ramped up nativist movement, leading – according to the Southern Poverty Law Center – to a 40 percent rise in the number of extremist anti-immigrant groups. Standing out among such groups is a new breed of border vigilantes. Shortly after the attacks, a former Los Angeles kindergarten teacher named Chris Simcox moved to Tombstone, Arizona, where he spent months camping out along the border. He claimed that this experience made him acutely aware of the threat that illegal immigration posed to national security. Soon after, Simcox purchased a small newspaper, the *Tombstone Tumbleweed*, which, in October 2002, became his launching pad for a "call to arms." Simcox announced the formation of a citizens' militia that would shame the federal government into securing the southern border. "It is a monumental disgrace," Simcox told the *Washington Times*, "that our government is letting the American people down, turning us into the expendable casualties of the war on terrorism."[12]

Simcox put his ideas into action by founding what he dubbed the Civil Homeland Defense, with the stated mission of assisting the Border Patrol in intercepting undocumented border crossers. In April 2005 he teamed up with a Vietnam veteran and ex-accountant named Jim Gilchrist to help form the Minuteman Project, adopting its name to evoke the citizens' militias of the American revolutionary era. Simcox went on to head the Minuteman Civil Defense Corps (MCDC). The Minuteman Project and the MCDC were soon joined by numerous subsidiaries and splinter groups that practiced varying degrees of vigilantism and that espoused varying levels of extremism. By 2007 there were 144 citizens' groups patrolling the southern border. They included such outfits as the Border Guardians, who specialized in burning Mexican flags and spouting vicious anti-Mexican rhetoric. In addition, advocacy groups with various anti-immigrant agendas – including anti-terrorism activists, the Christian Right, and white supremacists – have sprouted like mushrooms.

Simcox's call to arms was echoed with a vengeance on the political Right. The post-September 11 era witnessed the appearance of such works as Michelle Malkin's tellingly titled book *Invasion*, which lambasted bureaucratic boondoggles for allowing criminals and terrorists into the country and called for a wholesale "militarization" of the border with National Guardsmen "at least until 100,000 new Border Patrol and interior enforcement agents are trained and ready to be deployed."[13] Another notable anti-immigrant bestseller was Pat Buchanan's provocatively titled *State of Emergency: The Third World Invasion and Conquest of America*, published in 2006, which described recent immigration as nothing short of "the greatest invasion in history," and insisted on the notion – also subscribed to by the likes of Jim Gilchrist and other activists – that Mexicans were actively scheming to "reconquer" the southwestern United States.

Meanwhile, a number of recent events have helped to focus national attention on the issue of illegal immigration. Many of those events took place in Arizona, which seems to have replaced California as the hub of anti-immigrant sentiment. In Maricopa County, Arizona, Sheriff Joe Arpaio announced in 2006 that he would put together a posse of 100 deputies and other volunteers to patrol the desert to enforce a harsh anti-immigrant-smuggling law recently passed by the Arizona state legislature. Arpaio had a "tent city" built to house, in brutal and humiliating conditions, the hundreds of undocumented immigrants he arrested. Arpaio's methods have been widely criticized by human rights, anti-racist, and civil liberties groups, but as recently as 2007 he dodged a recall attempt and polls showed that 65 percent of Arizonans approved of him and his methods. As of this writing, Arpaio is the target of numerous lawsuits, is being investigated by the US Department of Justice, and has rapidly deteriorating relations with the local judiciary. He nevertheless remains a hero to many. In 2010 Minuteman founder Chris Simcox launched a campaign to unseat Arizona Senator John McCain, who in 2005 had co-authored an immigration bill with Senator Ted Kennedy that anti-immigration forces scorned as soft on immigration. When his campaign fizzled, Simcox threw whatever weight he had behind radio talk show host J. D. Hayworth, who boasts similar anti-immigrant credentials. McCain prevailed in an August 2010 primary, but only after spending $21 million and renouncing his own earlier efforts toward immigration reform. Also in 2010, the Arizona legislature passed, and the governor signed, a bill that required police to inquire into the immigration status of persons they detained. The bill aroused enormous controversy and condemnation, including national and international boycotts of the state, but it appears in fact to be closely akin to California's Proposition 187 – that is, a purely symbolic act, destined to have a negligible impact on actual illegal immigration.

While many anti-immigrant activists vehemently deny that they are "racist," they are inevitably linked to racist groups by commonality of interests and by their determination to identify immigrants – both documented and undocumented – with criminals and terrorists. Pro-immigration writers point out that rates of arrest and incarceration are actually significantly lower among immigrants than among citizens, and that only a tiny minority of prosecutions for immigration violations have any link to international terrorism (only 7 out of 37,765 in fiscal year 2004, and only 1 out of 26,771 in FY2003).[14] Occasionally, commentators on the issue let slip what they are really thinking. Take, for instance, right-wing television talk show host Bill O'Reilly who, in a 2008 interview with Republican presidential contender John McCain, accused the "far left" of defending immigrants in an attempt to "break down the white,

Christian, male power structure" in the United States. Or Pat Buchanan, who waxed nostalgic for the "country I grew up in," which was "89–90 percent white."[15] While certainly not all anti-immigration activists are racists, it seems fair to say that racial anxiety plays a large role in their worldview. They especially fear the so-called "browning of America."

While the anti-immigrant movement is loud and bellicose, most American citizens and politicians seem to be ambivalent on the issue (although the Republican Party's position appears to be hardening of late). Colorado Congressman Tom Tancredo sought the 2008 Republican presidential nomination by campaigning on a harsh anti-immigrant platform, but his campaign failed to gain traction. Organized labor and the national business community, at least as represented by the AFL-CIO and the Chambers of Commerce, have come to agree on a moderate policy that would include a path to legalization for illegal immigrants. And according to one recent poll, a solid majority of Americans (ca. 86 percent) support "comprehensive immigration reform" – though the pollsters did not specify precisely what that meant. A smaller, but still solid, majority (68 percent) said that, once the borders were "secured," employers punished, and criminals deported, they would support a path to citizenship for the 12 million or so undocumented immigrants currently living in the country illegally. Only 21 percent felt strongly that the solution to illegal immigration was to deny all benefits to illegal immigrants or to carry out mass deportations.[16] The poll's findings are likely not anomalous, for they have been supported by other recent polling.

Still, "comprehensive immigration reform," while apparently enjoying broad support, has proved elusive. George W. Bush called for immigration reform in January 2004, but expended little political capital toward promoting it. In 2007 the Senate considered legislation based largely on the 2005 initiative of Senators Edward Kennedy and John McCain, which offered a path to legal residency and created a guest worker program. The bill was severely diluted in an effort to get votes, but even so it was defeated.

In the meantime, Latino immigrants have greatly increased their presence in national politics. In late 2005 the House of Representatives passed the draconian Border Protection, Anti-Terrorism, and Illegal Immigration Act, better known as the Sensenbrenner bill, which would

Figure 5.1 The past two decades have witnessed a ferocious backlash against illegal immigration. Former Congressman Tom Tancredo, a leader of the anti-immigrant forces, addresses a rally while Minuteman founder Jim Gilchrist looks on. Washington, DC, February 2006. © Stephen Voss Photography.

have transformed illegal presence in the United States from a misdemeanor to a felony, threatened anyone giving aid to an undocumented person with up to five years in prison, increased the penalty for employing an undocumented worker to $7,500 for a first offense, and "expedited" the removal of apprehended undocumented immigrants. The Act was met with nationwide protests by Latinos, whose rallying cry – "*Hoy marchamos, mañana votamos*" ("Today we march, tomorrow we vote") – must surely have been heard by at least some politicians. The Sensenbrenner bill, which failed to pass the Senate, was likely a factor in causing applications for naturalization in 2006 to increase 54 percent over the previous year.

Sparking a similar response was a series of workplace raids carried out by Immigration and Customs Enforcement, which seemed to portend a more aggressive and more militarized approach to illegal immigration. ICE is the largest, most lavishly funded investigative unit in the Department of Homeland Security, absorbing a fifth of the DHS budget.

In the fall of 2006, ICE launched a series of raids on homes and work-places, ostensibly to arrest perpetrators of identity theft. In December 2006 more than 1,000 ICE agents carried out pre-dawn, commando-style raids at six Swift meatpacking plants in six different states, carrying off hundreds of people to detention centers. In the next few years immigrant detentions rose to more than 440,000 per year, becoming the fastest-growing part of the national prison system. On May 12, 2008, ICE carried out a notorious raid on a kosher meat plant in Postville, Iowa, that employed mostly Guatemalan workers. The raid, which involved two law enforcement helicopters, dozens of armed, flak-jacketed federal agents, and representatives from 16 local, state, and federal agencies, resulted in the arrest of 389 people. Although authorities justified the raid with the claim that the workers were guilty of identity theft, of 697 workers at the plant only one was found to have been using a Social Security Number that coincided with a reported identity theft. The raid harmed far more than undocumented immigrants: it devastated the little town of Postville, shrinking its population by nearly half, bankrupting the meat plant, dis-rupting kosher meat supplies, and causing hardship for regional livestock farmers. Most of the men arrested in the raid accepted deportation rather than face criminal charges, but some – mostly women – remain under a kind of house arrest, unable to work and supported by local charities.

In general, the raids wrought havoc with immigrant families, caused hardship for immigrants and citizens alike, and ultimately resulted in few prosecutions of businesses for using illegal labor. In 2008, of nearly 6,000 people arrested in raids, only 135 were employers or managers. Local police, meanwhile, complained that assisting in ICE raids diverted time and much needed resources from their regular law enforcement duties. Moreover, the raids are thought to have cost a whopping $13,000 for every person detained, not counting the legal costs of processing them.

Reports of illegal searches and seizures, violations of Fourth and Fifth Amendment rights, and abusive detention conditions have sparked outrage among immigrants and immigrant rights advocates. Bush's Attorney General, Michael Mukasey, in January 2009, issued the contro-versial ruling that immigrants do not have a constitutional right to consult a lawyer in deportation hearings, overturning a constitutional protection that immigrants had enjoyed for decades. It seems likely that the fallout from the raids will give fresh fuel to the already heated debate on immigration.

Epilogue and Conclusion

Mexico has witnessed a number of positive trends in recent decades. An ambitious family planning initiative begun in the 1970s has cut the birth rate in half; life expectancy has increased from 61 years to 70 years for men, and from 65 to 75 years for women; infant mortality has declined from 31 to 22 deaths per 1,000 live births; university enrollment has risen by 42 percent; and a new middle class has formed, which former Mexican Foreign Minister Jorge Castañeda calls "the single most important factor in the beginning of a reduction in ancestral Mexican inequality."[1] Moreover, since the year 2000 Mexico has gone from having an authoritarian single-party state to nurturing a robust, albeit imperfect, democracy (as if there were such a thing as a perfect democracy). US–Mexican relations were not warm during the presidency of George W. Bush, and the dominant perception among Mexicans still seems to be that "the United States [is] power-hungry, hypocritical, and anti-Mexican."[2] But there is some evidence that even this perception may have moderated a bit in recent years.

On a less cheerful note, however, violence and corruption remain very much a part of Mexican politics, and while democracy may have increased openness and transparency, it has also led to gridlock that has obstructed needed reforms. Mexico continues to have one of the lowest tax rates in the Western Hemisphere, making it impossible for the government to carry out basic infrastructure upgrades and provide essential social

Beyond Borders: A History of Mexican Migration to the United States
By Timothy J. Henderson
© 2011 Timothy J. Henderson

assistance. In order to become more competitive, Mexico especially needs to make drastic improvements in its neglected educational system. But Vicente Fox tried and failed to move such proposals through Congress, and his successor, Felipe Calderón, has hardly tried.

High hopes for NAFTA have been mostly frustrated. Annual economic growth between 1992 and 2007 was a severely anemic 1.6 percent per capita, domestic investment has been extremely low, and job creation has lagged badly. The peso crash of 1994 and the subsequent bailout forced Mexico to follow the prescriptions of international lenders, including cutting state spending and holding down wages. Such policies, coupled with a continuing oversupply of labor, has actually increased the gap between average wages paid in Mexico and the United States – precisely the opposite of what NAFTA's promoters promised.

The recession of 2008 hit Mexico especially hard, for it negatively affected the country's every source of legal revenue – tourism, oil, and remittances from emigrants in the United States. Tourism was dealt a blow by a swine flu epidemic that originated in Mexico, and by President Calderón's signature initiative – a hideously violent, all-out war on drug trafficking cartels that has cost the lives of some 24,000 people in four years. And since NAFTA linked Mexico's economy more closely than ever to that of the United States, the recession in the United States sent Mexico's economy into a tailspin. Mexico stood to lose up to 735,000 jobs in 2009, and even its unimpressive economic growth suddenly shifted into negative territory. Experts expect the economy to decline by around 7.5 percent.

The 2008 recession, along with drug violence and intimidation at the border, led to a sharp decline in Mexican immigration to the United States. According to Mexican census data, nearly a quarter of a million fewer people left for the United States in 2008 than did so in 2007, and researchers have amassed compelling evidence that walls and fences do not explain the drop. "If jobs are available, people come," one demographer stated simply. "If jobs are not available, people don't come."[3]

But at the same time, the recession has inspired few of the roughly 12.7 million Mexicans currently living in the United States to return to Mexico, even despite the scarcity of jobs. This phenomenon actually *might* have to do with increased border enforcement. Unemployment has hit Mexican immigrants hard, but the difficulties and expense of returning to the United States after a sojourn in Mexico have tended to persuade workers to remain in the United States, hoping for a quick economic recovery. Remittances – money sent by immigrants in the United States to their families back in Mexico – dropped by about 13.4 percent in 2009, causing severe hardship, especially for rural dwellers, some of whom count on remittances for up to 27 percent of their household budgets. Meanwhile, observers began to notice a surprising phenomenon: "reverse remittances," that is, money sent from families in Mexico to help sustain unemployed migrants in the United States.

In the United States the future of immigration reform is uncertain. The Obama administration has quietly altered or reined in several of the more bellicose policies of the Bush administration. It launched an overhaul of the immigrant detention system, which was costly and overloaded. It largely put an end to the Bush-era commando raids on work places, focusing instead on auditing companies so as to sanction employers who hire – and often exploit – undocumented workers rather than punishing the immigrants. The Obama Department of Homeland Security has relieved the infamous Sheriff Joe Arpaio of Maricopa County, Arizona, of federal authority to make arrests on charges related to immigration. It has shifted focus from simply deporting immigrants who are in the country unlawfully to trying to find and deport immigrants who have been implicated in serious crimes. And the administration has promised to pursue "comprehensive immigration reform" in the near future.

The prospects for such reform appear dim as of this writing. The Republican Party has shown little willingness to cooperate with the Obama administration on anything, and even President Bush was unable to interest his own party in undertaking comprehensive immigration reform. Many within the Democratic Party also oppose the kinds of reforms Obama appears to have in mind. The anti-immigration faction in Congress is grouped into the Immigration Reform Caucus, founded by anti-immigrant crusader Tom Tancredo. Of its 93 members, 6 are Democrats.

The kinds of policies that are usually listed under the heading of "comprehensive immigration reform" are not new. Nearly all have been tried before, and most have had little effect or have made the problem worse. Most reform packages contain a status adjustment for many of the undocumented immigrants already in the United States, increased border enforcement, and beefed up employer sanctions. Some versions also contain a guest worker program or an expansion of the number of legal visas made available to Mexico. In order to get anything past Congress, political considerations will mostly likely oblige the Obama administration, whatever its true inclinations, to make an obligatory show of "toughness" on the immigration issue, which means more expensive and ineffective border fences are almost sure to be part of any reform package.

A path to legalization for the undocumented Mexicans currently in the United States is essential and probably inevitable, despite the violent resistance the notion provokes on the Right. Even though the experience of IRCA indicates that legalization might well increase the volume of immigration, nearly all serious reform proposals include such a measure, for the alternatives are either morally reprehensible or fanciful. One alternative, of course, is the status quo, which leaves roughly 7 million Mexicans living in the United States without basic rights and protections and vulnerable to exploitation by unscrupulous employers, while at the same time undermining the whole notion of the rule of law.

Another alternative recommended by some anti-immigration activists is a wholesale round up and deportation of all of the 12 million or so undocumented immigrants in the country. This is sheer fantasy. Such a campaign would be unimaginably expensive – by one estimate, it would end up costing in the order of $250 billion[4] – and mostly likely impossible. Assuming it was attempted, it would certainly end up, like earlier such campaigns, deporting a fair number of legal immigrants and US citizens, destroying families in the bargain. Moreover, the sudden depositing of 7 million people into a Mexico already in economic distress might destabilize that country in ways that are difficult to predict. And, even if feasible, mass deportation would be only a temporary fix. Operation Wetback of 1954, presumably the model for such a mass deportation scheme, reduced illegal immigration for a few years, but only because it was accompanied by an expanded Bracero Program.

Some anti-immigrant activists advocate a program of "attrition through enforcement," by which they mean a concerted effort to deny undocumented immigrants access to virtually all of the amenities of civilized life, including not only welfare, but education, healthcare, housing, and identification. The idea would be to make the lives of the undocumented so miserable that they would depart voluntarily. Such a policy, apart from being inhumane, would likely be resisted by immigrants and many US citizens, making its prospects of success doubtful.

A good portion of the serious research on the illegal immigration issue has suggested that many of the objections to a legalization program – that newly legalized immigrants will displace citizens from jobs, depress wages, undermine US culture and political institutions, and generally set the country on the road to chronic conflict and penury – are extremely overblown. Some critics charge that legalizing the undocumented would reward lawbreaking and thereby undermine the rule of law. That charge reeks of hypocrisy, given the bizarre workings of the immigration system currently in force. A system more perfectly designed to breed disrespect for the law is hard to imagine. On the one hand, American employers, many wielding serious political clout, make clear to Mexicans that they are ardently wanted in the United States, the more the merrier. On the other hand, the US government provides Mexico with enough visas to meet only an infinitesimal portion of the demand, leaving illegal entry as the only option for Mexicans wishing to take the proffered jobs. The government also builds fences and walls that make both entering and leaving the United States a difficult, dangerous, costly proposition. And the mixed signals continue. Illegal immigrants have long been offered the possibility of "voluntary departure," a system wherein they may waive their right to a hearing and avoid detention by agreeing to leave at their own expense. They are thereupon sent to the nearest port of entry, with all parties tacitly understanding that they will shortly try to enter the country again, perhaps the same day.

Nor are mixed signals restricted to the border. President Bill Clinton's first two nominees for attorney general – the nation's top enforcer of the law – had to withdraw from consideration when it was discovered that they had employed undocumented immigrants as caretakers for their children. And all of this pales by comparison with the most long-lived and blatant hypocrisy of all, namely that employers of undocumented immigrants, whether through legal exemption or lack of enforcement, have almost never been held accountable for their role in the scheme – a role that logic would suggest is an infraction at least as heinous as entering the country without documents.

In the long term, the only thing that holds out any hope for success will be a leveling of the tremendous gap in wealth between the United States and Mexico. As the recent recession has shown, a serious economic downturn in the United States will cause a drop off in immigration, but greater prosperity in Mexico would obviously be preferable to permanent penury in the United States. Immigration policy should be pursued by the United States and Mexico working collaboratively, something that has only rarely been attempted. The timing is propitious, since Mexico, despite its resentment of many recent US policies, has expressed an unprecedented willingness to cooperate in gaining control over migration. Former Mexican Foreign Minister Jorge Castañeda has suggested the essential outlines of a bilateral agreement. Under his scheme, Mexico would commit to a three-part program. First, it would work to enforce its own immigration laws, which prohibit persons from leaving Mexico by anything other than the proper, legal channels. Second, in the prime sending areas, Mexico would seek to discourage emigration by establishing a program to reward families that have a male head of household present, and penalize those that do not. And third, Mexico would work to secure its southern border, which is currently a conduit for Central American migrants as well as drugs, guns, gangs, and a variety of other contraband, much of which eventually finds its way into the United States.

The United States would reciprocate by instituting a fair and rapid process for legalizing undocumented Mexicans, opening up new legal channels for temporary immigration, enforcing penalties on employers of undocumented workers, and upholding fair labor standards and anti-discrimination laws.[5]

Working in cooperation, the United States and Mexico could perhaps find ways to channel migrant remittances, which amount to about $23 billion a year, into areas that are most likely to enhance economic development and job creation in Mexico. The United States and Canada should also follow the lead of European countries, which from the 1960s through the 1980s invested generously in aiding the economic development of the poorer European countries – investment that the richer European countries, unlike the United States and Canada on the eve of NAFTA, viewed as a necessary prerequisite for the creation of a functional free trade system. This, of course, would require US capitalists to abandon the view of Mexico as a perennial supplier of cheap labor. To have any chance of success, it would also require Mexico to reform its tax system, upgrade its infrastructure, and improve its educational system. The idea would also have to somehow overcome what is sure to be vehement resistance by certain conservatives, for whom foreign aid is anathema. Still, it is hard to make a credible case that the billions currently being lavished on building fences and deporting undocumented workers would not be more effectively spent on trying to make life more agreeable for Mexicans living in Mexico.

Attaching "social clauses" to international trade agreements and concessions might further help the cause. Such clauses would oblige firms that invest in developing countries to honor internationally recognized standards on wages and working conditions, obstructing the tendency of such firms to scour the globe in search of the cheapest labor, and pitting, for example, Mexico against China in the quest for foreign investment and access to export markets – a situation often described as a "race to the bottom."

Whether rational immigration reform will be politically feasible seems doubtful at present. On the hopeful side, surveys have suggested that the American public has developed a more nuanced view of immigration, an appreciation that immigration is a complex issue that will not be solved by the kinds of policies that can be summed up on a placard or bumper sticker (i.e., "Send Them Home," "Secure Our Borders," "English Only," etc.). On the other hand, a significant and very assertive portion of the population remains fully addicted to the notion of such simple solutions without questioning their practicality or even possibility. These elements are sure to make themselves heard in upcoming debates about the issue.

For all its complexity, immigration is fundamentally an economic issue that cries out for economic solutions. The thought of tall, double-layer, reinforced fences and well-armed patrolmen standing guard at the southern border might give comfort to some Americans – though polls have showed that those Americans are in the minority – but there is no reason to suppose such barriers will be able to defeat the law of supply and demand. Supply and demand is a powerful law, and whether the objects in question are jobs, narcotics, or guns, prohibition has historically had a dismal record. That dismal record, of course, has never done much to dampen the enduring appeal of prohibition for some segments of society.

Americans think very differently about their northern and southern borders. The border between the United States and Mexico is a little more than half as long as the border with Canada and has only one third the number official entry points. The southern border is nevertheless guarded by 28 times more Border Patrol agents. Borders exist to protect affluence and privilege, as well as to protect and preserve distinctive cultures and practices. Canada's similarity to the United States – ethnically, socioeconomically, culturally, politically – makes it seem less a threat, even though if terrorists should want to enter the country across a border, the northern border would seem the more promising choice. The insistence on conflating Mexican immigration with terrorism and criminality surely reflects deep-seated anxieties about American nationhood that go far beyond a desire merely to protect "national security." In some segments of the American population, that anxiety will likely prove impervious to reason.

The right to emigrate – to leave one's native country – is enshrined as a basic principle in the United Nations' Universal Declaration of Human Rights. In the southern Mexican state of Oaxaca, where three out of every four people live in extreme poverty, where conditions have worsened since the enactment of NAFTA, and where a substantial portion of the population has left for the United States, people have taken to demanding another right: the right *not* to migrate – that is, to stay home and enjoy a modicum of comfort and dignity, free from exploitation. Mexico is rich in resources, and the very fact that emigration has taken place on such a grand scale over so many years proves that the Mexican people are, by and large, hardworking, resourceful, and enterprising. If the fruits of economic integration can be justly distributed, migration may one day become a choice rather than a necessity.

The system of migration from Mexico to the United States that has developed over the past century is unjust and cruel. It separates people from home, friends, and family; it deprives Mexico of some of its most energetic citizens; it obliges migrants to run unreasonable risks to reach their destination; and, presuming those migrants reach their destination, it leaves them with no protection or recourse against exploitation and abuse. This system was created principally by American business interests that felt their need for low-cost, low-skilled labor was best met by a large, unregulated, vulnerable foreign workforce. Those business interests have sustained the system for more than a century; their efforts have been aided by ongoing economic problems in Mexico, and by US politicians who seek to appease a variety of inflexible and antagonistic groups rather than trying to regulate the system for the maximum benefit of all concerned.

Fixing this dysfunctional system will be daunting, but my hope is that by providing an account of how it developed – over time and on both sides of the border – this book might help citizens and policy-makers see a more rational and productive way forward.

Notes

Introduction

1 *Personal Memoirs of U. S. Grant*, Vol. 1 (New York: Charles L. Webster, 1885), 53.

2 Studies of such matters are plentiful and the debate is ongoing, but a good place to start is Carol M. Swain, ed., *Debating Immigration* (Cambridge: Cambridge University Press, 2007). For an interesting and provocative attempts to debunk some myths, see also Eduardo Porter, "Cost of Illegal Immigration May Be Less Than Meets the Eye," *New York Times*, April 16, 2006; Jason L. Riley, *Let Them In: The Case for Open Borders* (New York: Penguin, 2008); and Aviva Chomsky, *"They Take Our Jobs!"* and 20 Other Myths About Immigration (Boston: Beacon Press, 2007).

3 Noah Pickus and Peter Skerry argue that the image of undocumented Mexicans "living in the shadows" is overdrawn, since many have obtained driver's licenses, joined unions, and some 10 percent own their own homes. But even according to their figures, nearly 60 percent lack health insurance and, if 10 percent own homes, presumably 90 percent do not. "Good Neighbors and Good Citizens: Beyond the Legal–Illegal Immigration Debate," in Swain, *Debating Immigration*, 95–113.

4 See Gilbert G. González and Raul Fernández, "Empire and the Origins of Twentieth-Century Migration from Mexico to the United States," *Pacific Historical Review*, Vol. 71, No. 1 (February 2002), 19–57, which argues that

Beyond Borders: A History of Mexican Migration to the United States
By Timothy J. Henderson
© 2011 Timothy J. Henderson

migration was spurred by American economic imperialism, so to view the push and pull as two distinct factors is to create a "false dichotomy."

1   Beginnings: 1848–1920

1 *Texas Journal of Commerce*, July 10, 1880.
2 Quoted in Fred Wilbur Powell, *The Railroads of Mexico* (Boston: Stratford, 1921), 110.
3 Ibid., 112.
4 Lawrence Cardoso, *Mexican Emigration to the United States, 1897–1931: Socio-Economic Patterns* (Tucson: University of Arizona Press, 1980), 29. *California Fruit Grower* quoted in Mark Reisler, *By the Sweat of their Brow: Mexican Immigrant Labor in the United States, 1900–1940* (Westport, CT: Greenwood Press, 1976), 6.
5 George is quoted in Carey McWilliams, *Factories in the Field: The Story of Migratory Farm Labor in California* (Boston: Little, Brown, 1939), 12; Marx is quoted in the same source, 56.
6 Henry George, *Our Land and Land Policy, National and State* (San Francisco: With & Bauer, W. E. Loomis, 1871), 37.
7 McWilliams, *Factories in the Field*, 4.
8 The calculations can be found in Manuel Gamio, *Mexican Immigration to the United States: A Study of Human Migration and Adjustment* (New York: Dover, 1971), 35–46.
9 Lawrence A. Cardoso, "Labor Emigration to the Southwest, 1916 to 1920: Mexican Attitudes and Policy," in George C. Kiser and Martha Woody Kiser, eds., *Mexican Workers in the United States: Historical and Political Perspectives* (Albuquerque: University of New Mexico Press, 1979), 19; Gamio, *Mexican Immigration*, 184.

2   Restriction, Depression, and Deportation: The 1920s and 1930s

1 Quoted in Mae M. Ngai, *Impossible Subjects: Illegal Aliens and the Making of Modern America* (Princeton: Princeton University Press, 2004), 24.
2 Quoted in Casey Walsh, "Eugenic Acculturation: Manuel Gamio, Migration Studies, and the Anthropology of Development in Mexico, 1910–1940," *Latin American Perspectives*, Issue 138, Vol. 31, No. 5 (September 2004), 126.

3   Madison Grant, *The Passing of the Great Race, or the Racial Basis of European History*, 4th edition (New York: Charles Scribner's Sons, 1922), xxxi.

4   *Mestizo* is also sometimes used as a sort of generic term for people of mixed race, not necessarily of Indian/European mixture.

5   Quoted in David G. Gutiérrez, *Walls and Mirrors: Mexican Americans, Mexican Immigrants, and the Politics of Ethnicity* (Berkeley: University of California Press, 1995), 54, 55.

6   Quoted in Abraham Hoffman, *Unwanted Mexican Americans in the Great Depression: Repatriation Pressures, 1929–1939* (Tucson: University of Arizona Press, 1974), 10.

7   Ngai, *Impossible Subjects*, 31.

8   Quoted in Francisco E. Balderrama and Raymond Rodríguez, *Decade of Betrayal: Mexican Repatriation in the 1930s*, revised edition (Albuquerque: University of New Mexico Press, 2006), 21.

9   Quoted in George Kiser and David Silverman, "Mexican Repatriation during the Great Depression," in George C. Kiser and Martha Woody Kiser, eds., *Mexican Workers in the United States: Historical and Political Perspectives* (Albuquerque: University of New Mexico Press, 1979), 50.

10 Manuel Gamio, *Mexican Immigration to the United States: A Study of Human Migration and Adjustment* (New York: Dover, 1971), 94.

11 Quoted in Ernest Galarza, *Merchants of Labor: The Mexican Bracero Story* (Charlotte: McNally and Loftin, 1964), 39.

12 Carey McWilliams, *Factories in the Field: The Story of Migratory Farm Labor in California* (Boston: Little, Brown, 1939), 225.

3   The Bracero Era: 1942–1964

1   Ernesto Galarza, *Merchants of Labor: The Mexican Bracero Story* (Santa Barbara: McNally and Loftin, 1964), 16.

2   Otey M. Scruggs, "Texas and the Bracero Program, 1942–1947," in George C. Kiser and Martha Woody Kiser, eds., *Mexican Workers in the United States: Historical and Political Perspectives* (Albuquerque: University of New Mexico Press, 1979), 88.

3   Quoted in Galarza, *Merchants of Labor*, 55.

4   Galarza, *Merchants of Labor*, 63.

5   Quoted in Stephen G. Rabe, *Eisenhower and Latin America: The Foreign Policy of Anti-Communism* (Chapel Hill: University of North Carolina Press, 1988), 16.

6   Quoted in Juan Ramon García, *Operation Wetback: The Mass Deportation of Mexican Undocumented Workers in 1954* (Westport, CT: Greenwood Press, 1980), 89.

7   Quoted in Garcia, *Operation Wetback*, 86.

8   Quoted in Otey M. Scruggs, "The United States, Mexico, and the Wetbacks, 1942–1947," *Pacific Historical Review*, Vol. 30, No. 2 (May 1961), 149.

9   García, *Operation Wetback*, 184.

10   Ibid., 225.

11   Ibid., 232.

12   Ibid., 230.

13   Galarza, *Merchants of Labor*, 183–197.

14   Luis González, *San José de Gracia: Mexican Village in Transition*, trans. John Upton (Austin: University of Texas Press, 1972), 243.

15   George M. Foster, *Tzintzuntzan: Mexican Peasants in a Changing World* (Boston: Little, Brown, 1967), 275–277.

16   Harry E. Cross and James A. Sandos, *Across the Border: Rural Development in Mexico and Recent Migration to the United States* (Berkeley: Institute of Governmental Studies, University of California, 1981), 43.

17   Wayne A. Grove, "The Mexican Farm Labor Program, 1942–1964: Government-Administered Labor Market Insurance for Farmers," *Agricultural History*, Vol. 70, No. 2 (Spring 1996), 314.

4   Illegal Immigration and Response: 1964–1990

1   On the negligible impact of maquiladoras on illegal migration, see Mitchell A. Seligson and Edward J. Williams, *Maquiladoras and Migration* (Austin: Mexico–United States Border Research Program, 1981); and Alberto Davila and Rogelio Saenz, "The Effect of Maquiladora Employment on the Monthly Flow of Mexican Undocumented Immigration to the US, 1978–1982," *International Migration Review*, Vol. 24, No. 1 (Spring 1990), 96–107.

2   Quoted in Julia Preston and Samuel Dillon, *Opening Mexico: The Making of a Democracy* (New York: Farrar, Straus and Giroux, 2004), 84.

3   Quoted in Henry C. Schmidt, "The Mexican Foreign Debt and the Sexennial Transition from López Portillo to De la Madrid," *Mexican Studies/Estudios Mexicanos*, Vol. 1, No. 2 (Summer 1985), 232.

4   Nora Lustig, *Mexico: The Remaking of an Economy*, 2nd edition (Washington, DC: Brookings Institution, 1998), 95.

5 Press release from the office of Herbert Lehman, quoted in Mae N. Ngai, *Impossible Subjects: Illegal Aliens and the Making of Modern America* (Princeton: Princeton University Press, 2004), 243.

6 AFL-CIO lobbyist Hyman Bookbinder, quoted in Daniel Tichenor, *Dividing Lines: The Politics of Immigration Control in America* (Princeton: Princeton University Press, 2002), 208.

7 Ibid., 247.

8 Quoted in Roberto Suro, *Watching America's Door: The Immigration Backlash and the New Policy Debate* (New York: Twentieth Century Fund, 1996), 14.

9 Quoted in Carlos Rico, "Migration and US–Mexican Relations, 1966–1986," in Christopher Mitchell, ed., *Western Hemisphere Immigration and United States Foreign Policy* (University Park: Pennsylvania State University Press, 1991), 248.

10 All quotes from Joseph Nevins, *Operation Gatekeeper: The Rise of the "Illegal Alien" and the Making of the US Mexico Boundary* (New York: Routledge, 2002), 63–64.

11 Antonia Hernández, quoted in Tichenor, *Dividing Lines*, 253.

12 Quoted in Tichenor, *Dividing Lines*, 250.

13 Quoted in Ngai, *Impossible Subjects*, 253.

14 Alan K. Simpson, "The Politics of Immigration Reform," *International Migration Review*, Vol. 18, No. 3 (Autumn 1984), 486–504.

15 Quoted in Rico, "Migration and US–Mexican Relations," 268.

16 "Memorandum for Lieutenant General Brent Scowcroft, US–Mexican Presidential Meeting, November 2, 1974." File scanned from the National Security Advisor's Memoranda of Conversation Collection at the Gerald R. Ford Presidential Library, http://www.fordlibrarymuseum.gov/library/document/memcons/1552833.pdf.

17 Echeverría, "Mexico's President Comments On Wetbacks In The United States." From the English-language version of President Luis Echeverría's second State of the Union Address delivered to Mexico's Congress on September 1, 1972, *Mexican Newsletter* No. 8 (September 1, 1972); reprinted in George C. Kiser and Martha Woody Kiser, eds., *Mexican Workers in the United States: Historical and Political Perspectives* (Albuquerque: University of New Mexico Press, 1979), 196.

18 The preceding discussion is greatly indebted to Rico, "Migration and US–Mexican Relations."

19 Paul R. Ehrlich, Loyh Bilderback, and Anne H. Ehrlich, *The Golden Door: International Migration, Mexico, and the United States* (New York: Ballantine, 1979), 333.

20 Quoted in Tichenor, *Dividing Lines*, 257.

21   Michael Fix of the RAND-Urban Institute, quoted in Aristide Zolberg, *A Nation by Design: Immigration Policy in the Fashioning of America* (New York: Russell Sage Foundation; Cambridge, MA,: Harvard University Press, 2006), 375.

5   Free Trade and Homeland Security: 1990–Present

1   Julia Preston and Samuel Dillon, *Opening Mexico: The Making of a Democracy* (New York: Farrar, Straus and Giroux, 2004), 187.

2   The quotation is from Lawrence Summers, US Undersecretary of the Treasury for International Affairs. Quoted in Andres Oppenheimer, *Bordering on Chaos: Mexico's Roller-Coaster Journey Toward Prosperity* (New York: Little, Brown, 1996), 230.

3   "UN Releases Controversial Study on Mexican Judicial System," SourceMex Economic News and Analysis on Mexico, http://www.allbusiness.com/ north-america/mexico/175329-1.html.

4   For example, see Rebecca L. Clark and Jefrey S. Passel, "How Much Do Immigrants Pay In Taxes?" Program for Research on Immigration Policy Paper PRIP-UI-26, Washington, DC: Urban Institute, 1993, which concluded that in California, immigrants contributed $12 billion per year more in taxes than they consumed in services, and that nationwide they contributed $28.7 billion more than they consumed.

5   Quoted in Sacha Feinman, "Drug Cartels Imperil Immigrants in the Desert," *Los Angeles Times*, July 19, 2009.

6   For a particularly thoughtful review, see Peter H. Schuck, "Alien Rumination: What Immigrants Have Wrought in America," in Schuck, *Citizens, Strangers, and In-Betweens: Essays on Immigration and Citizenship* (Boulder: Westview Press, 1998), 326–358.

7   This is a major theme of Douglas S. Massey, Jorge Durand, and Nolan J. Malone, *Beyond Smoke and Mirrors: Mexican Immigration in an Era of Economic Integration* (New York: Russell Sage Foundation, 2002).

8   Quoted in Carlos Salas, "Mexico's Haves and Have-Nots: NAFTA Sharpens the Divide," *NACLA Report on the Americas*, Vol. 35, No. 4 (January/February 2002), 33.

9   Paul Cooney, "The Mexican Crisis and the Maquiladora Boom: A Paradox of Development or the Logic of Neoliberalism?" *Latin American Perspectives*, Vol. 28, No. 3 (May 2000), 74.

10 Quoted in Jorge Castañeda, *Ex Mex: From Migrants to Immigrants* (New York: New Press, 2007), 78.

11 William Matthews, "Not-So-Secure Border Initiative: Critics Cite $6.5M-a-Mile SBInet's Many Problems, Technical and Otherwise," *Defense News*, 12 October 2009, http://www.defensenews.com/story.php?i=4321237&c=FEA&s=SPE (accessed January 4, 2010).

12 Quoted in Roxanne Lynn Doty, *The Law Into Their Own Hands: Immigration and the Politics of Exceptionalism* (Tucson: University of Arizona Press, 2009), 33.

13 Malkin, *Invasion: How America Still Welcomes Terrorists, Criminals, and Other Foreign Menaces to Our Shores* (Washington, DC: Regnery, 2004), 233.

14 Doty, *The Law Into Their Own Hands*, 55; Immigration Policy Center, *A Congressional Guide to Immigration: Answers to Tough Questions* (Washington, DC: Immigration Policy Center, 2009), 21; http://www.immigrationpolicy.org/sites/default/files/docs/FullMemberPacketWEB.pdf.

15 Quoted in Doty, *The Law Into Their Own Hands*, 55, 79.

16 Peter Brodnitz, Benenson Strategy Group memo, "Recent Polling on Immigration Reform," June 2, 2009, http://amvoice.3cdn.net/ea94778f39d6c895c3_zvm6beppq.pdf (accessed January 4, 2010).

Epilogue and Conclusion

1 Jorge Castañeda, *Ex Mex: From Migrants to Immigrants* (New York: New Press, 2007), 5.

2 Stephen D. Morris, "Exploring Mexican Images of the United States," *Mexican Studies/Estudios Mexicanos*, Vol. 16, No. 1 (Winter 2000), 106.

3 Jeffrey S. Passel, senior demographer at the Pew Hispanic Center, quoted in Julia Preston, "Mexican Data Say Migration to US Has Plummeted," *New York Times*, May 15, 2009.

4 Castañeda, *Ex Mex*, 173.

5 Castañeda, *Ex Mex*, 176–184.

Further Reading

General overviews of Mexican immigration to the United States are rare, especially ones that take the Mexican side of the equation into account. Such works include James D. Cockcroft, *Outlaws in the Promised Land: Mexican Immigrant Workers and America's Future* (New York: Grove Press, 1986); Harry E. Cross and James A. Sandos, *Across the Border: Rural Development in Mexico and Recent Migration to the United States* (Berkeley: Institute of Governmental Studies, University of California, 1981); and Paul R. Ehrlich, Loyh Bilderback, and Anne H. Ehrlich, *The Golden Door: International Migration, Mexico, and the United States* (New York: Ballantine, 1979). For an especially provocative interpretation – one that takes issue with the common view of Mexican immigration as responding to "push and pull" factors – see Gilbert G. González and Raul Fernández, "Empire and the Origins of Twentieth-Century Migration from Mexico to the United States," *Pacific Historical Review*, Vol. 71, No. 1 (February 2002), 19–57. David G. Gutiérrez considers immigration and ethnic relations in the United States in *Walls and Mirrors: Mexican Americans, Mexican Immigrants, and the Politics of Ethnicity* (Berkeley: University of California Press, 1995). A pair of anthologies that include valuable readings on the topic are David G. Gutiérrez, ed., *Between Two Worlds: Mexican Immigrants in the United States* (Wilmington: SR Books, 1996), and George C. Kiser and Martha

Beyond Borders: A History of Mexican Migration to the United States
By Timothy J. Henderson
© 2011 Timothy J. Henderson

Woody Kiser, eds., *Mexican Workers in the United States: Historical and Political Perspectives* (Albuquerque: University of New Mexico Press, 1979).

Histories of Mexicans in the United States are abundant. That story is told, with varying degrees of objectivity, in Manuel G. González, *Mexicanos: A History of Mexicans in the United States*, 2nd edition (Bloomington: Indiana University Press, 2009); Carey McWilliams, *North from Mexico: The Spanish-Speaking People of the United States* (New York: Greenwood Press, 1968); Rodolfo Acuña, *Occupied America: A History of Chicanos*, 7th edition (New York: Prentice-Hall, 2010); Juan González, *Harvest of Empire: A History of Latinos in America* (New York: Penguin, 2000); Stan Steiner, *La Raza: The Mexican Americans* (New York: Harper and Row, 1970); and Jack D. Forbes, *Aztecas del Norte: The Chicanos of Aztlán* (Greenwich, CT: Fawcett Publications, 1973).

Readers wishing to learn more about the history of Mexico have plenty of books to choose from, clearly too many to be listed here. A sampling of the available textbooks includes Michael Meyer, William Sherman, and Susan Deeds, *The Course of Mexican History*, 9th edition (Oxford: Oxford University Press, 2010); Colin MacLachlan and William Beezley, *El Gran Pueblo: A History of Greater Mexico*, 3rd edition (Upper Saddle River, NJ: Prentice-Hall, 2003); Douglas W. Richmond, *The Mexican Nation: Historical Continuity and Modern Change* (Upper Saddle River, NJ: Prentice-Hall, 2002); Alicia Hernández Chávez, *Mexico: A Brief History*, trans. Andy Klatt (Berkeley: University of California Press, 2006); and Jurgen Buchenau, *Mexican Mosaic: A Brief History of Mexico* (Wheeling, IL: Harlan Davidson, 2008).

General histories of immigration to the United States are also fairly abundant, especially those that focus on US immigration policy. Three fine surveys of US policy-making with regard to immigration are Daniel T. Tichenor, *Dividing Lines: The Politics of Immigration Control in America* (Princeton: Princeton University Press, 2002); James G. Gimpel and James R. Edwards, Jr., *The Congressional Politics of Immigration Reform* (Boston: Allyn and Bacon, 1999); and Aristide R. Zolberg, *A Nation by Design: Immigration Policy in the Fashioning of America* (Cambridge, MA and New York: Harvard University Press and the Russell Sage Foundation, 2006). Some specific aspects of the story are told by Mae N. Ngai in

Impossible Subjects: Illegal Aliens and the Making of Modern America (Princeton: Princeton University Press, 2004) and "The Strange Career of the Illegal Alien: Immigration Restriction and Deportation Policy in the United States, 19921–1965," *Law and History Review*, Vol. 21, No. 1 (Spring 2003), 69–107.

The best sources on the early years of Mexican immigration to the United States are Lawrence A. Cardoso, *Mexican Emigration to the United States, 1897–1931: Socio-Economic Patterns* (Tucson: University of Arizona Press, 1980), which is based on extensive work in Mexican archives; Mark Reisler, *By the Sweat of Their Brow: Mexican Immigrant Labor in the United States, 1900–1940* (Westport, CT: Greenwood Press, 1976), which treats the topic mostly from the US point of view; and Carey McWilliams, *Factories in the Field: The Story of Migratory Farm Labor in California* (Boston: Little, Brown, 1939). McWilliams, as the title suggests, focuses on California, still the most popular destination for Mexican migrants; the author was active in many of the events he narrates.

During the 1920s and 1930s, while heated and often ill-informed debates raged in the United States, several scholars began to take the phenomenon of Mexican migration seriously, and their works remain valuable. These include studies by Emory Bogardus, a sociologist associated with the University of Southern California, the most prominent of which is *The Mexican in the United States* (New York: Arno Press and the New York Times, 1970; originally published by the University of California Press, 1934). Mexican anthropologist Manuel Gamio was commissioned by the Social Science Research Council to study the topic in the mid-1920s. He produced two volumes: *Mexican Immigration to the United States: A Study of Human Migration and Adjustment* (New York: Dover, 1971), an objective study; and *The Life Story of the Mexican Immigrant* (New York: Dover, 1971), which contains personal stories of migrants. The most important work of the period was carried out by University of California economist Paul S. Taylor. Taylor interviewed more than a thousand people in California, Texas, Colorado, Pennsylvania, and Illinois, and eventually produced a series of eleven monographs titled *Mexican Labor in the United States*, published by the University of California at Berkeley between 1927 and 1934. For a nice appreciation of Taylor's work, see Abraham Hoffman, "An Unusual Moment: Paul S.

Taylor's *Mexican Labor in the United States* Monograph Series," *Pacific Historical Review*, Vol. 45, No. 2 (May 1976), 255–270.

Other important aspects of migration in the 1920s are addressed in William D. Carrigan and Clive Webb, "The Lynching of Persons of Mexican Origin or Descent in the United States, 1848 to 1928," *Journal of Social History*, Vol. 37, No. 2 (Winter 2003), 411–438; and Harvey A. Levenstein "The AFL and Mexican Immigration in the 1920s: An Experiment in Labor Diplomacy," *Hispanic American Historical Review*, Vol. 48, No. 2 (May 1968), 206–219.

The story of Mexican migrants in the Great Depression is told in two excellent books: Abraham Hoffman, *Unwanted Mexican Americans in the Great Depression: Repatriation Pressures, 1929–1939* (Tucson: University of Arizona Press, 1974); and Francisco E. Balderrama and Raymond Rodríguez, *Decade of Betrayal: Mexican Repatriation in the 1930s*, revised edition (Albuquerque: University of New Mexico Press, 2006). Some specific aspects of Mexican migration and Mexican labor in the United States are covered in Camille Guerin-Gonzales, *Mexican Workers and American Dreams: Immigration, Repatriation, and California Farm Labor, 1900–1939* (New Brunswick: Rutgers Unviersity Press, 1994); Gilbert G. González, *Mexican Consuls and Labor Organizing: Imperial Politics in the American Southwest* (Austin: University of Texas Press, 1999); and Zaragosa Vargas, *Proletarians of the North: A History of Mexican Industrial Workers in Detroit and the Midwest, 1917–1933* (Berkeley: University of California Press, 1993). Some interesting material on repatriation schemes in Mexico can be found in Casey Walsh, "Eugenic Acculturation: Manuel Gamio, Migration Studies, and the Anthropology of Development in Mexico, 1910–1940," *Latin American Perspectives*, Issue 138, Vol. 31, No. 5 (September 2004), 118–145; and Casey Walsh, "Demobilizing the Revolution: Migration, Repatriation and Colonization in Mexico, 1911–1940," Center for Comparative Immigration Studies, Working Paper No. 26, November 2000.

The Bracero Program has received considerable attention. The standard sources are Ernesto Galarza, *Merchants of Labor: The Mexican Bracero Story* (Santa Barbara: McNally and Loftin, 1964); Richard B. Craig, *The Bracero Program: Interest Groups and Foreign Policy* (Austin: University of Texas Press, 1972); and Manuel García y Griego, "The Importation of Mexican Contract Laborers to the United States, 1942–1964: Antecedents,

Operation, and Legacy," in Peter G. Brown and Henry Shue, eds., *The Border That Joins: Mexican Migrants and US Responsibility* (Totowa, NJ: Rowman and Allanheld, 1983), 49–98. Other works with more specialized angles include Kitty Calavita, *Inside the State: The Bracero Program, Immigration and the INS* (New York: Routledge, Chapman and Hall, 1992); and Erasmo Gamboa, *Mexican Labor and World War II: Braceros in the Pacific Northwest, 1942–1947* (Seattle: University of Washington Press, 2000). The story of *bracero* railroad workers is told in Barbara Driscoll, *The Tracks North* (Austin: University of Texas Press, 1999). The program was documented in photographs by the Hermanos Mayo photographic group, and their photos are collected in John Mraz and Jaime Velez Storey, *Uprooted: Braceros in the Hermanos Mayo's Lens* (Houston: Arte Publico Press, 1996). Deborah Cohen's *Braceros: Migrant Citizens and Transnational Subjects in the Postwar United States and Mexico* (Chapel Hill: University of North Carolina Press, 2010) was not published in time to be consulted for this study, but it promises to be a very significant contribution to the literature.

Various aspects of the program are addressed in numerous articles, among them Deborah Cohen, "Caught in the Middle: The Mexican State's Relationship with the United States and Its Own Citizen-Workers, 1942–1954," *Journal of Ethnic History*, Vol. 20, No. 3 (Spring 2001), 110–132; James F. Creagan, "Public Law 78: A Tangle of Domestic and International Relations," *Journal of Inter-American Studies*, Vol. 7, No. 4 (October 1965), 541–556; Wayne A. Grove, "The Mexican Farm Labor Program, 1942–1964: Government-Administered Labor Market Insurance for Farmers," *Agricultural History*, Vol. 70, No. 2 (Spring 1996), 302–320; Otey M. Scruggs, "Texas and the Bracero Program, 1942–1947," *Pacific Historical Review*, Vol. 32, No. 3 (1963), 251–264, reprinted in George C. Kiser and Martha Woody Kiser, eds., *Mexican Workers in the United States: Historical and Political Perspectives* (Albuquerque: University of New Mexico Press, 1979), 85–97; Otey M. Scruggs, "The United States, Mexico, and the Wetbacks, 1942–1947," *Pacific Historical Review*, Vol. 30, No. 2 (May 1961), 149–164; Ellis W. Hawley, "The Politics of the Mexican Labor Issue, 1950–1965," *Agricultural History*, Vol. 40 (1966), 157–176.

On Operation Wetback, see Juan Ramon García, *Operation Wetback: The Mass Deportation of Mexican Undocumented Workers in 1954*

(Westport, CT: Greenwood Press, 1980) and Kelly Lytle Hernández, "The Crimes and Consequences of Illegal Immigration: A Cross-Border Examination of Operation Wetback, 1943–1954," *Western Historical Quarterly*, Vol. 37, No. 4 (Winter, 1006), 421–444. Illegal immigration during the *bracero* era is addressed by the President's Commission on Migratory Labor, *Migratory Labor in American Agriculture: Report* (Washington, DC: US Government Printing Office, 1951); and Julian Samora, *Los Mojados: The Wetback Story* (Notre Dame: University of Notre Dame Press, 1971).

Some valuable sources on the "Mexican Miracle," especially with respect to agriculture, are Roger D. Hansen, *The Politics of Mexican Development* (Baltimore: Johns Hopkins University Press, 1971); Cynthia Hewitt de Alcantara, "The 'Green Revolution' as History: The Mexican Experience," in Ernest Feder, ed., *Gewalt und Ausbeutung. Latein-amerikas Landwirtschaft* (Hamburg: Hoffmann und Campe, 1973), 473–495; W. Whitney Hicks, "Agricultural Development in Northern Mexico, 1940–1960," *Land Economics*, Vol. 43, No. 4 (1967), 393–402; and Rodolfo Stavenhagen, "Social Aspects of Agrarian Structure in Mexico," in Rodolfo Stavenhagen, ed., *Agrarian Problems and Peasant Movements in Latin America* (Garden City, NY: Doubleday, 1979), 225–270.

An excellent account of Mexican views of the migration issue after the end of the Bracero Program is Carlos Rico, "Migration and US–Mexican Relations, 1966–1986," in Christopher Mitchell, ed., *Western Hemisphere Immigration and United States Foreign Policy* (University Park: Pennsylvania State University Press, 1991), 221–284. On US politics and policy in the run up to the Immigration Reform and Control Act of 1986, see Alan K. Simpson "The Politics of Immigration Reform," *International Migration Review*, Vol. 18, No. 3 (Autumn 1984), 486–504. A critical view of the impacts of the IRCA legislation can be found in Douglas S. Massey, Jorge Durand, and Nolan J. Malone, *Beyond Smoke and Mirrors: Mexican Immigration in an Era of Economic Integration* (New York: Russell Sage Foundation, 2002), one of the best sources on the contemporary state of Mexican immigration. For highly readable accounts of recent developments in Mexico, see Andres Oppenheimer, *Bordering on Chaos: Mexico's Roller-Coaster Journey Toward Prosperity* (Boston: Little, Brown, 1996) and Julia Preston and Samuel Dillon, *Opening Mexico: The Making of a Democracy* (New York: Farrar, Straus and Giroux, 2004). Economic changes in Mexico since the 1980s are analyzed in Nora Lustig, *Mexico: The Remaking of an Economy*, 2nd edition (Washington, DC: Brookings Institution Press, 1998); James M. Cypher, "Developing Disarticulation within the Mexican Economy," *Latin American Perspectives*, Vol. 28, No. 3 (May 2001), 11–37; Paul Cooney, "The Mexican Crisis and the Maquiladora Boom: A Paradox of Development or the Logic of Neoliberalism?" *Latin American Perspectives*, Vol. 28, No. 3 (May 2001), 55–83; Carlos Salas, "Mexico's Haves and Have-Nots: NAFTA Sharpens the Divide," *NACLA Report on the Americas*, Vol. 35, No. 4 (January/February 2002); *Mexican Workers Since NAFTA*, *NACLA Reports on the Americas*, Vol. 39, No. 1 (July/August 2005), Demetrious G. Papademetriou, "The Shifting Expectations of Free Trade and Migration," in Carnegie Endowment for International Peace, *NAFTA'S Promise and Reality: Lessons from Mexico for the Hemisphere* (Washington, DC: Carnegie Endowment for International Peace, 2003), 39–59; Susan Kaufman Purcell and Luis Rubio, eds., *Mexico Under Zedillo* (Boulder: Lynne Rienner Publishers, 1998); and Michele Waslin, "Immigration Policy in Flux," *NACLA Report on the Americas*, Vol. 25, No. 3 (November/December 2001), 34–38.

On barricade building and its effects, see Joseph Nevins, *Operation Gatekeeper: The Rise of the "Illegal Alien" and the Making of the US–Mexico Boundary* (New York: Routledge, 2002); Joseph Nevins and Timothy Dunn, "Barricading the Border," *NACLA Report on the Americas*, Vol. 41, No. 6 (November/December 2008), 21–25; Timothy Dunn, *Blockading the Border and Human Rights: The El Paso Operation that Remade Immigration Enforcement* (Austin: University of Texas Press, 2009); Wayne Cornelius, "Death at the Border: The Efficacy and 'Unintended' Consequences of US Immigration Control Policy, 1993–2000," Center for Comparative Immigration Studies, University of California–San Diego, Working Paper 27, 2001; Tony Payan, *The Three US–Mexico Border Wars: Drugs, Immigration, and Homeland Security* (Westport, CT: Praeger Security International, 2006); Peter Andreas, *Border Games: Policing the US–Mexico Divide* (Ithaca: Cornell University Press, 2000); and Stephanie Innes, "Nature Trumps Border Seal," *Arizona Daily Star*, September 24, 2006.

Several works are devoted to examining the recent rise in nativism in the United States. These include Robin Dale Jacobson, *The New Nativism:*

Proposition 187 and the Debate over Immigration (Minneapolis: University of Minnesota Press, 2008); Roxanne Lynn Doty, *The Law into Their Own Hands: Immigration and the Politics of Exceptionalism* (Tucson: University of Arizona Press, 2009); Kent A. Ono and John M. Sloop, *Shifting Borders: Rhetoric, Immigration, and California's Proposition 187* (Philadelphia: Temple University Press, 2002); and Kitty Calavita, "The New Politics of Immigration: 'Balanced-Budget Conservatism' and the Symbolism of Proposition 187," *Social Problems*, Vol. 43, No. 3 (August 1996), 284–305.

The "new geography" of Mexican immigration is the topic of Victor Zuñíga and Rubén Hernández-León, eds., *New Destinations: Mexican Immigration in the United States* (New York: Russell Sage Foundation, 2006).

The ICE raids of recent times are recounted in Antonio Olivo, "Immigration Raid Leaves Damaging Mark on Postville, Iowa," *Los Angeles Times*, May 12, 2009; Roberto Lovato, "Building the Homeland Security State," *NACLA Report on the Americas*, Vol. 41, No. 6 (November/December 2008), 15–20; Renee Feltz, "A New Migration Policy: Producing Felons for Profit," *NACLA Report on the Americas*, Vol. 41, No. 6 (November/December 2008), 26–30; Nigel Duara, William Petroski, and Grant Schulte, "Claims of ID Fraud Lead to Largest Raid in State History," *Des Moines Register*, May 12, 2008; and Annette Fuentes, "Report: ICE Raids Chilled Civil Liberties, Violated Constitution," *New American Media*, June 20, 2009.

Several works have been produced to recount the personal experiences of Mexican immigrants, beginning with Manuel Gamio's *The Life Story of the Mexican Immigrant*, mentioned above. Other contributions to this field include Marilyn P. Davis, *Mexican Voices/American Dreams: An Oral History of Mexican Immigration to the United States* (New York: Henry Holt, 1990); Rubén Martínez, *Crossing Over: A Mexican Family on the Migrant Trail* (New York: Henry Holt, 2001); and Sam Quinones, *Antonio's Gun and Delfino's Dream: True Tales of Mexican Migration* (Albuquerque: University of New Mexico Press, 2007).

Finally, one recent book is essential reading: Jorge Castañeda's *Ex Mex: From Migrants to Immigrants* (New York: New Press, 2007). Casteñeda provides a short, useful overview of the history of Mexican migration to the United States, but what makes his book especially invaluable is his account of his work on immigration issues during his stint as Mexico's Foreign Minister from 2000 to 2003. Casteñeda makes a number of excellent suggestions for resolving the problem of illegal Mexican immigration, though he is less than sanguine about the prospects for sensible reform.

Index

Beyond Borders: A History of Mexican Migration to the United States
By Timothy J. Henderson
© 2011 Timothy J. Henderson